Alan Joh

Left Standing

Nigel Cawthorne

© Nigel Cawthorne 2014

Nigel Cawthorne has asserted his rights under the Copyright, Design and Patents Act, 1988, to be identified as the author of this work.

First published by Endeavour Press Ltd in 2014.

Table of Contents

Introduction

In the middle of November 2014, with less than six months to go before a general election, leader of the opposition Ed Miliband scored the worst poll rating of any party leader since records began. Miliband shrugged and said: "What does not kill you makes you stronger."

According to *The Times*, the remark acknowledged that an attempted coup involving a number of Labour frontbenchers to top Miliband and install Alan Johnson in his place had failed. This was partly because Johnson had already refused the job. Only the day before, he had announced that he would never pitch for the leadership.

"I have never stood for the leadership of my party – and for the avoidance of doubt, regardless of the circumstances, I never will," he said. "Ed Miliband will lead us into an election that I am convinced we can win. It was my decision to walk away from frontline politics, not Ed's. The position of Labour leader has been vacated twice during my time as a member of parliament. Both times I chose not to stand. I happen to think that a better person took this onerous role on each occasion."

But some still had their doubts. Politicians have been known to change their minds. Some even back, apparently unwillingly, into the limelight. However reluctant to take the top job, they can usually be persuaded that the party – or even the country – needs them.

Alan Johnson is eminently qualified for the role as party leader. Elected to parliament in 1997, he has served as Home Secretary, Health Secretary, Education Secretary and Shadow Chancellor of the Exchequer. By contrast, Ed Miliband entered parliament in 2005 and served in the lesser government posts of Minister for the Cabinet Office, Chancellor of the Duchy of Lancaster and Secretary of State for Energy and Climate Change, before he was elected leader of the Labour Party.

Miliband is a committed Brownite, having worked as an advisor in the Treasury before joining Brown's cabinet. Johnson has served in government under both Blair and Brown.

The two men could not be more different. Miliband is a North London intellectual. His father, a Belgian-born Jew of Polish origin, was a Marxist academic. Ed and his brother David learnt their politics over the dinner table in Primrose Hill, then Ed went on to study at Oxford, the London School of Economics and Harvard. Johnson was born in Notting Hill, now the gentrified home of some Tory grandees, but then a slum, riven by race riots in the 1960s. He left school at fifteen, became a postman and worked his way up through the Union of Communication Workers to become its General Secretary, before becoming an MP.

Alan Johnson is old-school Labour with a genuine working-class background. He supported David Miliband in his bid to become leader of the Labour Party after the resignation of Gordon Brown.

After serving just three-and-a-half months as Ed Miliband's Shadow Chancellor, he resigned for personal reasons.

Since then, he has declined Ed's offers to return to the Shadow Cabinet. Asked if he would consider a role in the Cabinet if Miliband won the 2015 election, he said: "I would be more interested, but I am not gagging for it."

No matter what he says, many politicians and pundits regard him as the Labour leader – or even Prime Minister – in waiting.

Nigel Cawthorne

Bloomsbury, December 2014

www.nigel-cawthorne.com

Chapter One – The Wilds of West London

Alan Johnson was born on 17 May 1950 in Paddington General Hospital. His father, Steven Arthur Johnson, was a lance corporal in the British Army when he married Lilian May Gibson at Kensington Registry Office in January 1945. It was a low-key affair with, it appears, a single witness. The Registry Office was still swathed in barbed wire as a wartime precaution.

The bride – and later Alan's mother – Lily had been born in Liverpool in May 1921, the second of a family of ten, two of whom had died from pneumonia after contracting measles. Lily's grandmother had died at the age of forty-two. Her mother also perished at that age from cervical cancer.

By then the Gibsons had moved to a semi-detached house in a new council estate in Anfield. It had three bedrooms, a bathroom with an inside lavatory, electricity and gardens front and back. For a working-class family in the 1920s, this was heaven.

Nevertheless, for Lily, there were difficulties. While her mother was giving birth to her younger siblings, she was expected to help run the household. A clever girl, she was also supposed to be studying for a scholarship. Then, in the increasingly overcrowded conditions, she contracted rheumatic fever which damaged her heart. It also led to her being hospitalized with St. Virus Dance, the involuntary jerking of the limbs. The only cure, then, was to be strapped to the bed frame which rattled with her spasms. As a result, she was berated by the other patients who were trying to sleep.

Despite these trials, she won her scholarship, but could not take up her place when her father refused to pay for her school uniform. Forced to leave school early, she took a job in the Co-op. Then, during the war, she had joined the NAAFI – the Navy, Army and Air Force Institutes that provided recreational facilities for enlisted men – and left Liverpool for good.

While little over five feet tall, Lily had grown to be a ravishing red head. She got engaged to an older man who had contracted tuberculosis and died. On the rebound, she was waiting to be demobbed when she met Alan's father at dance in 1944.

Steve was a musician. He told Lily that he had been offered a job by the big band leader Bert Ambrose, but turned him down as Steve refused to learn to read music. Self-taught, he played the piano entirely by ear. A natural showman, he wore a pair of white gloves when he played in the NAAFI and had a reputation as a ladies' man.

Lily should have known better, but the war was ending and everyone was fired with optimism. Steve was a Londoner and that is where they would make their home. But as a scouser Lily was made to feel like an outsider in Notting Hill and remained self-conscious about her Liverpool accent for the rest of her life.

After the war, Steve looked for work as a painter and decorator, but he was feckless and could not hold down a job for long. Instead he supported his habits of drinking, gambling and smoking by playing the piano at parties, weddings and, in the evenings and at Sunday lunchtimes, around local pubs.

Their first child, Linda, came along in 1947. This was before the foundation of the National Health Service the following year. Linda was just 5lbs 4oz at birth, while Alan, who came along two years after the establishment of the NHS, was a healthy 10lbs. But, at birth, his umbilical cord was twisted around his neck. The difficult birth took its toll on Lily's already fragile health. Afterwards, as it would have been dangerous for her to have any more children, she was sterilized.

The baby boy was christened Alan, after the 1940s' film star Alan Ladd, and he was given the middle name Arthur, after his father. The family were then living in one room in a housing trust property in Southam Street, next to the railway lines at the back of Paddington Station. The slums there had been condemned fifteen years earlier but not even the Luftwaffe had knocked them down.

When Alan came along, the family moved into two rooms on an upper floor. They used one room as a bedroom, the other as a living room. There was no electricity. Lighting was provided by gas mantles – or, more often than not due to their poverty, tiny makeshift candles that were little more than a blob of wax with a wick in it. The gas was provided by putting a shilling in the meter.

In the evening, a lamplighter would arrive on his bike to light the streetlights outside the communal front door. There was a single squalid lavatory in the backyard with newspaper torn into squares as lavatory paper and a cistern that froze in the winter. Rather than use the lavatory on cold dark nights, they kept a bucket in the bedroom. Consequently, the tiny flat stank of urine – or worse. Washing was done in the sink, though clothes were sent out to the "bagwash" when they could afford it.

Before the gentrification of Notting Hill Gate, the area was officially designated North Kensington, but known locally as Kensal Town – or just The Town. Since the 1980s, estate agents have expanded the boundaries of Notting Hill and former dilapidated properties have been spruced up and sold to incoming middle-class families. Well served by the underground, the area is handy for Westminster and the City.

Alan's father boozed and gambled most of his money away. He contributed little to the household budget. So despite her poor health, Lily took jobs as a cleaner and a general dogsbody in the well-to-do houses of South Kensington and Ladbroke Grove. Her pay barely covered the rent and the meagre meals that she scraped together for the children. Food was in short supply generally. Rationing was still in force until Alan was four. Their staple diet was bread, butter and eggs, though sometimes there was nothing to eat but bread and dripping. At best, living was hand to mouth. Johnson remembered spending his childhood in an almost constant state of gnawing hunger. As a result, when Steve came home well-nourished and drunk, there would be a row that would sometimes end in violence.

In winter, Lily would scavenge coal for the fire. The children would sleep under mountains of old clothes for warmth. Conditions were little better in the summer. As the coal fire had to be used for cooking and hot water, it remained lit even on the hottest summer's day. They had no fridge to put food in. Milk had to be kept cool by standing it in a bowl of water and butter consigned to the coolest corner of the pantry, which was nothing more than a tiny cupboard on an outside wall, ventilated by an air-brick. As a result, the place was infested with flies, cockroaches, earwigs, beetles and all kinds of other insects.

Like Lily, Steve had not been brought up in such squalor. Alan recalled being taken by his father to visit his Nanny Johnson who lived with her youngest son, Uncle Jim, in Delgano Gardens. She had a flat in one of the blocks provided by the trust established by the American philanthropist George Peabody. Light and breezy, it was free of bugs, damp and the smell of decay. It had an indoor lavatory, a bath in the kitchen and even a carpet in the front room, along with a comfy sofa. Alan particularly remembered going there as a toddler because his father had held his hand. It was the only time he could remember them having physical contact – at least of a tender sort.

As post-war austerity lifted, Steve got an office job. Like most working-class men of that era, Steve turned out in an immaculately clean suit on a Sunday. It had been pressed with a flat-iron heated on the fire and his shoes had been polished and shined. While he headed off on his own, Lily would take the two children to play on what they called the The Debry – a bombsite remaining from the Blitz. Much of the area was filled rubble. There were other dangers. The railing around the recesses that allowed light into basements had been removed to make armaments. Instead they were fenced off ineffectively with sheets of corrugated iron.

On a Sunday, Steve would go and play the piano in the pub, before returning home for his Sunday dinner. Back then, the pubs were only open at a lunchtime on a Sunday from 12 until 2 pm. They would close all afternoon, open again at 7, and close at 10.30. The shops, too, were closed on a Sunday, though costermongers laden with shellfish, and a man with a horse and cart with a huge barrel of vinegar on the back toured the streets. As well as a condiment for the cockles and whelks, vinegar was used as a cure-all for cuts and bruises.

While Lily believed in God, they did not go to church on a Sunday. Nevertheless there were some observances at home. For example, it was considered sinful to play cards on the Sabbath. Beyond the teachings of the Church of England, Lily had a profound belief in astrology – not that the predictions she found *Old Moore's Almanack*, the monthly horoscope magazine *Prediction* or the *Daily Sketch* ever seemed to do her any good. None of this made any sense to Alan, who was an unshakeable atheist from an early age.

The children would go out either with their father or their mother – never the two together. Sometimes Steve would take them to visit his friends Ted and Elsie. Their children were of a similar age and Alan and Linda would play with them in the yard behind the flats. One day when Ted, a lorry driver, was away, Linda returned to the flat and walked in to find Steve in bed with Elsie.

When Lily discovered what had been going on, there was a huge row. This was overheard by the children and most of the neighbourhood. Steve then went to live with Elsie. When he returned home six months later, Elsie was pregnant and returned to Ted, who agreed to bring up Alan's half-brother David as his own. However, when Steve did not keep up the child-support payments he had promised, Ted came round and knocked him to the ground.

Despite everything, Lily took Steve back. It was important back then that children were seen to have two parents. Apparently, she still loved Steve and hoped he would change. In an attempt to make a fresh start, she arranged a family holiday in Liverpool, the first time Lily had returned there since the war.

They went by coach, with the kids kitted out in new clothes provided by loans from the Provident. But this only added to the burden of debt Lily had accumulated by getting things on tick at local stores.

Lily's mother was long dead and she did not get on with her father who was a martinet, but the trip was an opportunity for her to get together with her brothers and sisters, and their spouses. Steve managed to spoil the atmosphere by flirting with her sisters, upsetting both them and their husbands, and while Lily took the children around the places she had known as a child and to the seaside at New Brighton, Steve returned to his old ways, spending most of his time away from the family in the local boozers. The reconciliation was a failure.

Back in London, Steve spent more time away from home, disappearing for weekends to the seaside or taking time to travel down to Kent to play the piano for the hop-pickers. Still, little of the money he earned came into the household and Lily continued struggling to make ends meet. The children were dressed in second-hand clothes from the street market in Portobello Road and there was little food on the table. Only rarely would there be enough money left for the kids to get sixpence pocket money on Saturday.

Things got a little better when Alan started school at Wornington Road Infants' where he and Linda qualified for free school meals. Supremely conscious of the value of a good education, Lily had enrolled the two children at the local library. By the time they started school, both of them could already read.

When Alan was six, the family was moved down the street to a ramshackle apartment where they had three rooms and a gas cooker on the landing. This provided much needed heat in the winter. There were few cars on the roads in those days and kids could play in the street. Given the cramped accommodation and the state of the sanitation, adults and children alike preferred to spend a lot of the time outdoors, whatever the weather. However, before the Clear Air Acts of 1956 and 1960, they had to contend with the pea-souper fogs, which were actually smogs cause by the smoke from coal fires. It was dangerous to breathe the air and everything was covered in a thin layer of grim. Even so, Lily and other housewives spent hours scrubbing their front steps, turning them gleaming white in the gathering gloom.

While the building they had moved to was just as damp and dilapidated as the one they had left, Alan and Linda now had their own bedroom which they shared. It was on a landing also occupied by another family. The new place had electricity provided, like the gas, by a coin-operated meter. Despite these improvements, there was no heating in the bedroom, so before bedtime Lily would pop an earthenware hot-water bottle into the bed to warm the linen sheets. Otherwise the room, particularly the lino floor, was freezing. It was not unusual in those days to find frost on the inside of the window panes.

Lily's dream came true when the family was offered a council house. But it was out in the new town being built at Crawley in Sussex thirty miles to the south and Steve refused to move out of Notting Hill.

If the children managed to save up sixpence, they would head for the pie-and-mash shop or the sweet shops where they would buy homemade fizzy pop. Another favourite was the German bakers. They could not afford to buy anything there, but would nourish themselves on the smell of fresh-baked doughnuts and bread.

In those days, almost all adults smoked. Steve rolled his own, while Lily cut her factory-rolled cigarettes in half with an old razor blade, but still she would smoke them with the panache of a movie star.

Once a week, she would doll herself up, doing her hair and putting on her make-up in a broken mirror, and go to the pictures. Linda would be left in charge of her younger brother. When Lily returned, she would tell them of what she had seen on the silver screen. Though this was Lily's one indulgence, Steve resented the few pennies she spent on the cinema, though, on the rare occasions he backed a winner, the family saw none of the proceeds. Until 1960, off-course betting was illegal in the UK. Nevertheless Steve sent the children to place his bets with a nearby bookmaker, though they were never trusted to collect his winnings, if there were any.

Sometimes Steve would take the children with him when he was playing the piano at a wedding. This was a treat. They were particularly proud of him when he played at the children's Christmas party held in nearby Westbourne Grove. There they got Christmas presents, usually a book, which they treasured.

Otherwise Steve spent most of the day in bed and, though there was a decrepit piano in the flat, he made no effort to teach his children to play. Indeed, he kept it locked. They were also denied access to the music he kept on his collection of old shellac 78s as they had no record player. The only entertainment at home came from a radio that Lily rented.

Like the rest of the adult population of Britain in the 1950s, Steve and Lily did the pools and listened intently to the football results being read out on the wireless at five o'clock on a Saturday afternoon. In 1957, Lily won £90, the equivalent of £2,000 today. She used the money to make down payments on furniture and treats for the kids. Soon she was unable to keep up the payments and the kids spent much of their childhood dodging the tallyman. Eventually, most of what she had bought had to be returned.

However, they managed to retain a small, portable Dansette record player and an acoustic guitar, which Alan was determined to master. Though they could not afford to buy any new records, they could at least listen to Steve's old 78s.

Chapter Two – Family Break-up

By her early thirties, Lily was already prematurely middle-aged. Though her posh employers still gave her expensive hand-me-downs, she rarely appeared without her floral over-all and headscarf that were then the uniform of the charlady. Despite their poor diet, she had filled out and her face was lined and careworn.

Her doctors recommended rest, but she could not afford to give up her char work. As a result of overwork, she spent the Christmas of 1957 in hospital. On Christmas Eve, Steve disappeared and failed to return. On Christmas Day, alone and abandoned, the children found the Christmas hamper Lily had saved up for. After stuffing themselves with sweets, they decided to cook the chicken they found in it. Stuffing the gas meter with a few precious coins, they lit the oven and put the chicken in. However, they had not realized that they were supposed to unwrap the chicken first. The plastic wrapping melted, giving off acrid fumes and rendering the meat inedible. Further catastrophe was averted by the young Irishwoman who lived in the next landing and came running to the rescue.

After feeding themselves the best they could with the vegetables they had cooked, they set off to walk to Paddington General Hospital. Steve was waiting outside and warned them not to tell their mother that he had not come home – otherwise, she would get upset and die, he said. For the half-hour visiting time, they kept by the pretence that the three of them had had a nice Christmas dinner together. Afterwards, Steve did not come home with them. He did not return for another two days.

Lily was eventually sent home with orders to rest, but within a few weeks she had picked up fresh charring jobs. While she cleaned and scrubbed, the children were left to play in Kensington Gardens with sandwiches wrapped in waxed paper from sliced loaves. They had strict instructions not to talk to strangers and to take shelter in one of the museums on Exhibition Road if it rained. The Victoria and Albert Museum, the Science Museum and, particularly, the Natural History Museum became regular haunts.

Alan and Linda were only left to their own devices out of necessity. Otherwise, Lily bought them up with a firm hand. She was not against giving them a slap. They ran errands for neighbours and were commended for their manners.

While Lily's marriage had plainly been a disaster, she was determined to stick at it. A stigma was still attached to separation and divorce. But the children were conscious that there was something wrong with their parents' relationship, particularly compared with those of the parents of friends.

One particular friend was Tony Cox. He and Alan had met at Wornington Road Infants' School and moved on to Bevington Primary together. Tony's father Albert, in Alan's eyes, was an outstanding example of a decent, hardworking man, who looked after his wife and family and still wore his army beret with pride as a memento of his wartime service in the Royal Engineers. In peacetime, he worked as an engineer on the London Underground, while his wife worked in a fish-and-chip shop in Shepherd's Bush.

In the Coxes' home in Latimer Road, Alan experienced unimaginable luxury. It was warm and clean and they had a whole room where they neither ate nor slept. The whole family had a cooked breakfast every morning and their diet was supplemented with vegetables grown on Albert's allotment. He was a provider. What's more, they had a bookcase that contained a collection of second-hand classics, along with an *Encyclopaedia Britannica*. But, like Steve's piano, it was kept under lock and key. Unlike Alan and Linda, neither Tony nor his sister Carole were interested in reading. Despite repeated hints, Alan was denied access to this treasure trove too.

One interest Alan and Tony shared was collecting the cards that came with sweets, cigarettes and packets of tea. They were swapped or competed for in the playground. This was strictly segregated, with the girls confining their activities to skipping and innocent games involving bouncing balls. Only Linda stood out as something of a tomboy. She was allowed out with her skipping rope to play in the road, while Alan played with his model cowboys and Indians at home.

There were dangers for boys on the streets. At the age of six, Alan had his treasured collection of bus tickets stolen by an older boy. There were fights outside pubs and gangs of toughs roamed the streets. Steve tried to teach Alan to box to defend himself, and although Lily tried to protect him, Alan ended up black and blue.

Steve never used corporal punishments to discipline the young Alan, but he was beaten regularly at school. That was the norm back then.

While Lily liked to keep Alan safe at home, he was allowed out in the company of Tony Cox, who had a spare bike which he lent Alan – until he ran into a young woman coming out of a shop. Tony was also accomplished with his fist, while Alan sought to avert any fight by affecting to look tough. Neither that, nor Tony's fighting ability, were any good when Alan was seized in a headlock by a man in his twenties who was clearly deranged. Tony and their companion Dereck Tapper, the son of one of the recent West Indian immigrants to the neighbourhood, could do nothing as the youth threatened to slice Alan's face open with a piece of glass. Nevertheless, they stood by him until he could make his escape.

At the time, Notting Hill was notorious for the slum-landlord Peter Rachman. He packed West Indians – who were otherwise denied rooms by the offensive and ubiquitous sign that read: "No Blacks, No Irish, No Dogs" – into the overcrowded and inadequate accommodation, charging them extortionate rents. The immigrants also had to suffer the predations of the local Teddy Boys. Once Lily had to give refuge to one young white woman who had the temerity to go out with one of the black men.

In August 1958, an argument between a white woman and her Jamaican husband sparked a full-scale race riot that lasted six days. Over 140 people were arrested with nine white youths given exemplary sentences of five years in jail and fines of £500.

20

The Notting Hill riots were part of the young Alan's political education. Oswald Mosley, leader of the British Union of Fascists in the 1930s, returned to the streets there as part of the "Keep Britain White" campaign. Lily had no time for him. Her one political icon was Emmeline Pankhurst, founder of the suffragettes.

Nine months after the riots, she tried to intervene when a young black man was murdered by a white gang. Lily knew the man who delivered the fatal blow, but she did not give his name to the police, fearing retaliation. By then she had enough troubles of her own.

Tension grew at home when Linda passed her eleven-plus, which would allow her to go to a grammar school rather than the fearful local Sir Isaac Newton Secondary Modern. As a reward, Lily bought her a dog from Battersea Dogs' Home. Steve refused to have it in the house. When he was there, it had to be chained up in the back yard, whatever the weather.

On one freezing day, he came home unexpectedly – and far from sober – to find the dog in the house. In the ensuing fight, Linda attacked him with a knife, before running off with the dog. She was found hours later out on the open spaces of Wormwood Scrubs. Even Lily realized that this marked the end of any pretence of family life.

Much later in life, Linda revealed her untold suffering at that the hands of their father.

"He had been sexually abusing me since I was about four years old," she said. "It began one Sunday morning when I hopped into bed with mum and dad. Mum got up to make a cup of tea and Alan

21

was asleep in his cot. That was how it started. He would say it was because he loved me."

She was also outspoken about Alan's suffering at the hands of his abusive father.

"Alan was often the victim of Dad's drunken rages," she said. "Dad would pretend he was boxing with him, but the punches were real and hard. He told Alan he was a wimp and he should toughen up and learn to fight, punching as he spoke. Alan was always very brave and would try to fight back but would sometimes cry, which would make me so angry. Then Mum would intervene and get a wallop, too."

At the time, Australia was keen to attract fresh immigrants from the UK and were offering passage for £10. Lily suggested to the kids that the three of them should seek a better life down under. But while Alan and Linda were keen to escape from their father, they were adamant they were not leaving London.

Soon after, Steve walked out. Lily and the children came home one Saturday afternoon to find his meagre possessions and battered suitcase were gone. Alan was just eight years old. He and his older sister were ecstatic. But Lily sat down and wept.

The following day, she went to the pub where Steve played on Sunday lunchtime. There was no sign of him. His family also closed ranks. Lily was blamed for not having been a better wife to him and none of them would tell her where he was. After a while, gossip reached her that Steve had gone to live with Vera, the barmaid he had spent the previous Christmas with. No one knew where. Or so they said.

Finally, Southam Street was scheduled for demolition and Lily and the children were rehoused in Walmer Road, nearer Wormwood Scrubs and Shepherd's Bush. By then Alan was nine and Linda twelve, so the housing trust gave them a four-room flat so that the kids could have separate bedrooms. It also had a kitchen and Lily persuaded the trust to install a bathroom in the a squalid basement, though hot water for the bath still had to be heated on a gas ring. But money was tight and, on the rare occasions they had a bath, they had to share the water. They still had to share an outside lavatory with everyone else in the building. This one had no light.

Despite being rehoused, Lily's mood did not lift and Alan and Linda would hear her sobbing at night. For the children, this was almost as bad as the rows and fights they had overheard when Steve was still with them. She found some comfort when Linda moved into her bedroom with her. This allowed her bedroom to be turned into a living room, complete with a three-piece suite from the Salvation Army, where she could entertain her new friends from Fulham County Grammar School.

Despite the doctors' advice, Lily continued cleaning. She also took a job in a tobacco kiosk, then a café, further supplementing her income doing piece work varnishing wooden toys at home. Soon there was enough coming in to rent a television. Nevertheless, groceries still had to be bought on tick. When further credit was denied, Linda volunteered to work in the shop until the bill was paid off.

Lily decided that she wanted a divorce, so that if Steve could be tracked down, he would be liable to pay her maintenance. But first she had to find him. Meanwhile she returned to hospital for another long stay. Her heart condition, it seemed, was getting worse.

Then her luck changed. Thinking she was alone in one of the flats she cleaned in Notting Hill, she broke down crying. One of the young tenants overheard her and persuaded her to tell him what was wrong. It turned out that he was a journalist and offered to track Steve down for her. He took the simple expedient of phoning the pub where Vera had used to work, saying that he worked for an insurance company and had some money for her. He then visited the address in Dulwich he had been given for her and confirmed that Steve was living there.

The journalist's brother, who also lived in the flat, was a solicitor who, pro bono, obtained a divorce for her, along with a maintenance order for £6 10 shillings a week. A postal order for that amount began arriving every Friday, though payments soon tailed off. This curtailed such treats as fish and chips, and their diet largely returned to potatoes roasted in dripping, bubble and squeak and other left overs. Sometimes they were reduced to eating breakfast cereal twice a day, or bread floating in beef stock.

Nevertheless, with the advent of the 1960s, the family were seized by the new mood of optimism. Linda was doing well at school. Now it was time for Alan to sit his eleven-plus – his mother had ambitions for him to become a draughtsman. It was regular indoor work and you got to wear a suit.

For young Alan, though, there were distractions. Apart from cubs and an attempt to learn to swim that left him with a lifelong fear of water, there were the attractions of a fellow pupil named Linda Kirby. But all attempts to win her affections failed embarrassingly.

Where Alan did excel was his knowledge of the hit parade. Even his music teacher was impressed and, while money was still coming in from Steve, Alan and Linda even bought the latest 45s. Lily encouraged them. They saw Lonnie Donegan in pantomime at the Chiswick Empire and Cliff Richard and the Shadows at the London Palladium. She also bought Alan a crystal set so he could listen to Radio Luxembourg. Even at the age of six or seven, he was writing his own songs and was learning to play the guitar with Bert Weedon's instruction manual *Play in a Day*. His musical ability was the one thing he ascribed to his inheritance from his father.

Alan's other passion was football. He was a Queen's Park Ranger's fan, another thing he inherited from Steve though his father never took him to a match or even talked about football with him. However, he had left behind the QPR handbook from 1947-48, the season they had been promoted, which Alan repeatedly re-read. Lily gave him the money to go to Loftus Road, along with Tony Cox and his father Albert. She later paid for his subscription to *Charles Buchan's Football Monthly*.

He was also a fan of Enid Blyton's Famous Five and the cowboy book *Shane* and became so besotted with the novel's tall, dark hero that he was sorely disappointed when he saw the 1953 film version, starring his short, blond namesake Alan Ladd.

With Tony Cox and other friends, Alan played football and cricket in the streets of Kensal Town. Sometimes they explored the exotic reaches of Kensington Gardens and Holland Park, when peacocks roamed free. Otherwise there was a blasted heath of Wormwood Scrubs with its glowering prison to the west.

The rumour was that there had once been an army camp there. In their fertile – if rather confused – imaginations, British prisoners of war had been held there and tortured by the Japanese. One night, five of them set out to investigate. Among the bunkers, they found a tunnel. It was down there, they believed, that British troops had been incinerated in ovens by their merciless captors. With some trepidation, they entered, believing they were the first to have explored the death camp.

That expedition marked the end of childhood. This fearless band of brothers was about to be broken up by the education system that then sought to separate the sheep from the goats at the age of eleven.

Chapter Three – Big School

Alan Johnson passed his eleven-plus, but others failed and were sent to the dreaded Sir Isaac Newton Secondary Modern. While well-heeled parents were happy to see their children go to the new-style comprehensive in Holland Park, Lily was determined that Alan should go to a grammar school. That, she believed, was the way out of the life of limited opportunities to which she had been consigned.

The nearest grammar school did not even offer him an interview. Another, over the river in Battersea, looked down their nose at him. However, he did get into the Sloane School in Chelsea, along with Tony Cox and Dereck Tapper. This was perhaps due to the progressive views of its veteran headmaster or, more likely, Johnson thinks, because there was a shortage of pupils in the area as the denizens of Chelsea prefer to send their offspring to public schools.

Lily managed to buy a second-hand uniform. Social Services supplied his shoes and, along with free school meals, he was given free travel as the school was more than three miles away.

Johnson hated Sloane Grammar School. It was an enduring embarrassment to be picked out as one of the kids entitled to free school meals. Worse, the school was just five hundred yards from Stamford Bridge and most of the boys were Chelsea supporters.

Tony Cox flourished there. Despite the overt racism of the day, even Dereck Tapper excelled, going head to head in the gym with

Malcolm Macdonald who went on to play football for England. Dereck went on to university and acted at college.

Johnson was more bookish, watching documentaries in the geography block during break time and beginning a life-long love of the work of P.G. Wodehouse. He joined the school choir and sung the school productions of operas.

With her growing children becoming less of a burden, Lily also sought to make a new life for herself. At the behest of the brothers who had organized her divorce, she looked through ads in the lonely-hearts column of the local paper. She met one of the respondents in a nearby pub and, the following week, invited him home. It was vital, the children were told, that they made a good impression on him.

After Steve had left, Lily had taken a screwdriver to the lock on the piano. When her new beau arrived, he regaled them with robust renderings of popular hymns. The kids responded with a cappella versions of show tunes. He then recommended Alan try out for the choir at Westminster Cathedral, revealing that he was a Catholic. That was the last Lily saw of him.

Linda continued working at the local grocery store. She was now bringing regular money into the household and took charge when Lily made increasingly frequent sojourns in hospital.

Trouble ensued when Linda started seeing boys. Lily tried to impose strict rules on any courtship but as, when she was not in hospital she was out working, these could not be easily enforced. She gave way when Linda started dating a fifteen-year-old named Jimmy Carter who worked with his father as a rag-and-bone man.

The problem was when he came round he smelt of horse manure and Lily insisted that he take a bath to quell the stench. It was Jimmy who introduced Alan to smoking cigarettes.

Alan was hit in the eye in an accident in the school gym. The injury did not seem serious, but he managed to persuade his mother to keep him off school for four months. This put an added strain on her finances as she had to provided his meals, rather than have him stuff himself for free at school. He filled his time playing his guitar, inventing his own football league and producing his own soccer magazine called *Soccer News*. By the time he returned to school he was well behind and never caught up academically.

When the money from Steve dried up completely, Linda and Jimmy went to confront Steve who, reluctantly, paid some of what he owed. Vera then announced that she was pregnant. When Lily heard about this, she insisted that Alan go and see his father too, if only to keep in contact with his half-sister when she came along. Alan resolutely refused, though Linda continued to see him to force money from him and see her half-sister Sandra. It was only much later that Alan realized Linda's real motive was to try and protect Sandra from what she had gone through.

Jimmy's older brother Johnny, a milkman, gave Alan a Saturday job, which was then extended to cover the Sunday-morning round. His job was to collect the empties and pick up the money settling each household's weekly bill. For lunch, Alan and Johnny shared a Swiss roll, washed down with a pint of milk. They collected from some of Rachman's more run-down establishments. One of them was 10 Ruston Place, which had previously been Rillington Place where at least seven women had been murdered by John Reginald Christie in the early 1950s.

Johnson earned 10 shillings a week. Lily refused to take any of it. As money was always tight, she had also taught the children to keep their eyes on the ground. One day, Alan found nearly ten shillings in coins on the pavement outside a betting shop. As he could no longer go and seen QPR on a Saturday, the money he did not save was spent on football publications.

Back at school, Johnson played football as goalkeeper for his house. In this capacity, he faced Malcolm Macdonald, losing his place in the team after letting in five goals. Despite this humiliation, he looked forward to football practice. This involved a trip to the school's playing fields in Roehampton and got him away from school for an afternoon. It was all the more welcome as the playing fields were shared with Carlyle Grammar School for Girls.

In the summer of 1962, Johnson went on holiday, visiting in Denmark courtesy of the Children's Country Holiday Fund. On the crossing, they were hit by a storm and everyone was seasick. They stayed in an agricultural college and were taken on improving trips to the Lurpak dairy and the Lego factory. Also on the trip was the bully who had stolen his box of bus tickets when he was six. He now demanded the Danish kroner Johnson had been given as pocket money.

Johnson would have been reluctant to break the unwritten rule and grass the bully up to a teacher. But the students running the trip were not teachers. They beat the bully until he confessed, then hung him upside down until the stolen money came cascading from his pockets. Other children were warned that they could expect the same treatment if they bullied or stole.

The rest of the holiday Johnson compared to an Enid Blyton adventure. The English boys played endless internationals against Danish boys. This gave them the opportunity to show off in front of the girls in their party. Soon Johnson was going on long country walks holding hands with Edna, who was from a council estate in Whitechapel. They kissed and promised to stay in touch when they got back to England, but after another choppy voyage home they never saw each other again. Back in London, Lily, who met the boat train at Liverpool Street, wanted to know why every other kid was carrying a Lego set. Alan had been given one at the factory too, but had traded his for twenty cigarettes.

While he had been way, Lily had put an ad in the lonely-hearts column of the *Kensington Post*. As a result, she met Ron, a builder who owned a bungalow in Romford. Linda and Alan took against him, but Lily appeared accommodating, perhaps thinking that he could save her from the squalid conditions they were still living in. She agreed that they would go to his house for Christmas. He would provide the food; she would cook. But the bird he had bought was a goose. Lily had never even seen a goose before. Preparing it was a nightmare. Then, when it was in the oven, it caught fire. The meal was a disaster and, in the heat of the moment, Ron called her a stupid woman. As there were no trains or buses on Christmas Day, they had to stay the night. After Ron had driven them to station the following day, Lily never saw him again.

This curtailed young Alan's amorous opportunities too. While at Ron's house, his flirtatious daughter had invited him to visit her in her bedroom. It was an invitation that he did not take up, but suspected that Linda's boyfriend Jimmy, who had also seen the note, might have gone in his place. Soon after Linda explained the facts of life to him. The details appalled him, so perhaps it was best that he had not gone.

At school, Alan's favourite subject was English, where the class read George Orwell's *Animal Farm*. His English teacher also taught Religious Education, spending the lessons railing again racial segregation in South Africa. Having seen racism first-hand in Notting Hill, Alan was an easy convert to the anti-apartheid cause, though not to Christianity. Under the guidance of his English teacher, Alan also took to the stage in the school play.

Another new teacher also helped foster Alan's burgeoning political awareness. He was a Hungarian who had fled his homeland when Soviet tanks had crushed the uprising in 1956. He was a socialist, he said, not a communist, and explained the difference.

Alan had another long period off school after a near-fatal appendicitis, which was only caught in the nick of time. He spent a fortnight in hospital listening to the radio. This was where he first heard the Beatles' "Please Please Me". They were a favourite because they came from his mother's hometown. Here, at last, was home-grown talent, not a pale imitation of an American act. Alan was hooked.

Chapter Four – The Loss of Lily

Alan returned from hospital during the severe winter of 1962-63 in their freezing flat. It was the coldest winter since 1740. Every day, he had to trundle an old pram rescued from the tip round to the local coal merchants where the coal was still hauled by magnificent carthorses. The flat now possessed a two-bar electric heater, but it used too much electricity to be kept on for long.

As always, Lily insisted that Alan ask for the coal on tick, something that acutely embarrassed him. When this was refused, he had just enough cash to buy enough coal to keep the fire in the back room lit for a day, with a few extra lumps to be saved for Sunday when the coal merchants was closed. On the trip, he kept his eyes peels for other lumps to scavenge.

January 1963 was the coldest month since 1814 and the country was brought to a standstill by snow, ice and free fog. No football could be played, so the pools companies had to set up a panel to generate the results to keep them in business.

By March, when the thaw set it, Alan was passed fit for school. That May, a week before his thirteenth birthday, he overcame his enduring antipathy for Chelsea and went to Stamford Bridge to see the great Stanley Matthews, who was then playing for Stoke City in the twilight of his career.

Linda and her friends had become Mods, while Alan, like others of his generation, had discovered the records of black American R&B, such as B.B. King, Bo Diddley, John Lee Hooker, Howlin' Wolf and Muddy Waters, who had been all but forgotten in their own country. This music formed the backbone of the "British invasion" of the United States in 1964.

Alan, though, was a particular fan of Chuck Berry and bought American imports in a record store in Roehampton. These were borrowed by Linda's sharp-suited friends, earning her little brother inordinate respect. As soon as he could afford it, Alan was determined to become a Mod.

At school, Alan was surrounded by middle-class boys desperate to rebel. He had nothing to rebel against. In fact, thanks to the Beatles and kitchen-sink dramas on the stage and television, it was becoming fashionable to be working class. This gave him enough clout to form a band, the Vampires, who rehearsed in the basement of classmate Colin James's home in Parsons Green. It was also a place they could innocently entertain girls.

In the early 1960s, being in a band was the thing to do. Everyone wanted to jump on the bandwagon. One of the other boys at Sloane Grammar was Steve Hackett, who went on to become lead guitarist with Genesis and the supergroup GTR.

The Vampires sought further inspiration in the 100 Club in Oxford Street, Soho's Marquee Club and the Crawdaddy Club in Richmond. They saw the Rolling Stones, Georgie Fame and the Blue Flames, the Pretty Things, the Yardbirds and, later, Rod Stewart.

They began growing their hair long and customizing their school blazers with six-inch vents – the latest Mod fashion – inviting a caning from a disapproving headmaster. They also began hanging around out the World's End pub in King's Road, where the Rolling Stones were said to drink, but they never saw them there.

Alan and Colin had planned to take a holiday hitchhiking along the south coast. That was what rebellious youth did in those days. But instead they were persuaded to join the rest of Colin's family in a house-swap in Sussex. There Alan read *Goldfinger* in a single sitting. He was just hitting puberty when the country was engulfed in the Profumo sex scandal, some of which took place nearby in Notting Hill.

Lily's health was deteriorating and her GP petitioned the Housing Department to find her a council house as a medical priority. Linda quit school to get a job and bring in more money, while finding time to train as a nurse. Then Lily was told of a new procedure that might alleviate her heart condition. Without this ground-breaking operation, she would not live much longer, she was told. However, as it meant she would be hospitalized for at least three months, she refused.

Despite her determination to keep on working and Linda's contribution, Lily fell ever deeper into debt. She took to playing bingo in the forlorn hope of improving her lot with a big win.

With Johnny Carter, Alan began delivering paraffin two nights a week to bring in extra money. As a result, he stank of the stuff. But as part of the deal, he got a pie and chips on the way home. The money he earned was spent on records and paperback detective novels.

Linda's new boyfriends, the manager of a local electrical shop, introduced Alan to the records of Bob Dylan who immediately became his latest hero. Soon he could recite the words of Dylan's songs off by heart. He also had the album *Green Onions* by Booker T. and the MGs.

Both the gas and the electricity had been cut off when Linda went out on a date. Alan, who had been left at home in the freezing flat to keep an eye on his mother, grew concerned about her. When Linda came home, Lily was delirious and cried out to Steve, cursing him. The doctor was called. He summoned an ambulance.

With Lily in hospital again, sixteen-year-old Linda did her best to try and handle the family's calamitous financial situation. She made arrangements for the gas and electricity to be turned on again and was rehired part-time by the shop where she had earlier paid Lily's slate. The shopkeeper, hearing of their dire circumstances, gave them a box of groceries.

Now Lily had no choice. Without radical heart surgery, she would die. What's more, she would have to stay in the hospital until the operation was done. It was months away. Linda and Alan were careful who they told of their situation, fearing that they would be taken in to care or – worse – have to go and live with Steve. Besides the Vampires were too busy trying to cover the latest Beatle's single. Then came the news that President Kennedy had been assassinated.

Over Christmas, local families and shops rallied round. Lily wanted to come home to be with her children for the holiday, but the doctors would not let her return to the unhealthy conditions there. So Linda and Alan spent Christmas Day alone again. This time, they remembered to unwrap the chicken before they cooked it.

They visited the hospital on Christmas afternoon. Lily was cheerful, promising them that they would have their own home the following year. On the way home, Linda told Alan that Lily still had not signed the consent form for the operation and asked him what he thought. Alan said that, if the operation was Lily's only chance, she should go ahead. When they got home, the woman upstairs gave them sandwiches in front of a blazing fire. It was the first time Alan had tasted turkey.

Left to his own devices, Alan's circle of friends grew. They all seemed to come from families that were loving and stable – and a good deal better off. He gained a reputation of being bookish, so much so that the German mother of a friend gave him a copy of Dante's *Inferno*, which he found unfathomable, though he did not let on.

The night before her operation, Lily wept openly in front of other people. It was the only time Alan remembered her doing so. She still had not signed the consent forms. She was afraid. At forty-two, she was now at the age both her mother and grandmother had died. Linda did her best to persuade her to sign the papers.

The following day, after the operation, Lily was in intensive case in a medically induced coma. A week later, after a second operation, her kidneys failed. Linda, who herself was devastated by the news, then had to tell Alan. He was unable to take in what he was being told and found himself unable to shed a tear. It was only years later that he found he could cry at the thought of his precious, long-dead mother.

As always, Linda took charge. She informed Lily's family in Liverpool, took time off from work and told Alan's school that he would not be back there for a while. There was the death certificate to handle, the birth certificate to find and the funeral arrangements to organize. The cost was fortunately covered by an insurance policy. In the mortuary, they discovered that Lily's wedding ring had to be cut off her finger and they were handed her dentures. With the advent of the NHS, it was common among working-class people to have all their teeth taken out and replaced with false ones. Linda and Alan also had to make the rounds to inform Steve's family, but declined any offers of help.

Lily was to be cremated. Aunt Jean and Uncle George would be coming down from Liverpool for the funeral and offered to take the children back with, but Linda and Alan did not want to go.

They stayed at the Coxes until the funeral where, at long last, the book case was unlocked and Alan was lent a leather-bound copy of *David Copperfield*. When their aunts and uncles arrived, they were in shock. They had known nothing of Lily's heart condition and were doubly shocked by the living conditions she had been reduced to in Walmer Road.

Friends and family were not given to displays of emotion. However, on the Saturday before Lily's funeral, after they had finished the milk round, Johnny Carter, who had somehow acquired a large collection of musical instruments, asked Alan to pick one. Alan chose a Vox. It was his first electric guitar and Linda's new boyfriend provided an amplifier.

Wearing a black knitted tie that Steve had left behind, Alan attended the funeral at All Souls, Kensal Green with his sister and a large contingent of scousers. In the cemetery they spotted Steve. At his request, Linda left Alan with him for a few moments. Steve made his apologies and gave Alan a key ring with a little football attached to it. It was the last they ever saw of each other.

Afterwards, Linda and Alan went to stay in Liverpool for a week, but then returned to London, determined to go on living together on their own in Walmer Road. However, they soon received a notice addressed to her mother that the building was going to be demolished as it was no longer fit for human habitation. She was to be rehoused in a three-bedroom semi in Welwyn Garden City.

This meant they could no longer stay on in Walmer Road and they were too young to take over the house in Welwyn. Though Linda had been one of the mainstays of the family for years, she was still considered to be a child. They were told that she would be sent to Dr Barnado's, while Alan would be put in foster care. Linda refused to budge, insisting that they stayed together. After all, they had been taking care of themselves for years.

The council reluctantly gave way and agreed to rehouse them, provided that they were visited regularly by a social worker and an adult stood guarantor. Uncle Jim agreed to do that and they were offered a flat at the top of a tower block in Hammersmith. When they visited it, they found it in a worse state than Walmer Road and they refused it. Eventually they were offered a two-bedroom maisonette at the south end of Wandsworth Bridge. It had a bathroom and an indoor toilet. For Linda and Alan this was opulence.

Steve had offered to help with the rent, but his contribution soon dried up. Nevertheless, Linda somehow managed. The neighbours were hostile though, resentful that a flat had been given to two teenagers when, in their eyes, other families were more deserving. As a result, the flat was vandalized and regularly burgled. But they could not risk complaining to the police or their social worker in case the authorities reverted to their plan to put them in care.

Slowly Alan began to enjoy school. The new English teacher engaged the pupils with contemporary literature and took them to the theatre and musicals. He encouraged Alan's interest in reading and introduced him to new writers he thought he would enjoy. Nevertheless, Alan wanted to leave school as soon as possible. Linda was against this and turned up at parents' evenings to tell the teachers so. But Alan was determined to get on with his career as rock star.

Chapter Five – The Road from Rock

When he left school at the age of fifteen in July 1965, another grammar-school boy named Harold Wilson was prime minister and Alan began taking an interest in politics – particularly the radical reforms the Labour government were pushing through. When he got his first proper job as a postal clerk at the headquarters of Remington Razors in High Street Kensington, he bought *The Times* to read on the way to work.

After six months, he got another job in the Tesco's warehouse in Hammersmith with Andrew Wiltshire, a friend from school who owned a drum kit. With Danny Curtis, a childhood acquaintance from Notting Hill, they formed a band called The Area. Danny had a van to transport the gear and put an ad in *Melody Maker*. This bought them a lead guitarist named Tony Kearns from Chester and bassist Ian Clark, a Scottish music student at London University.

The line-up had just got together when Alan's Vox was stolen in one of their frequent break-ins. But Lily had left £40 for Alan, which Linda had intended to give him when he was older. He used the money to buy a red Höfner Verythin from a shop in Soho.

Soon they were playing Wednesday nights at the Pavilion pub opposite Wormwood Scrubs, even though they were too young to drink there. They also supported Fifth Dynasty and the Symbols, who had a couple of minor hits in the 1960s, which took them to gigs in other pubs, clubs and colleges.

While Alan's musical career seemed to be taking off, Linda got married. Her new husband found them a house in Watford. This lost them the maisonette in Wandsworth and Alan returned to Notting Hill. He moved in with the Coxes and shared a room with his old friend Tony, who now had a Lambretta and a parka with "The Who" emblazoned on the back.

While they were committed to the band, Alan hedged his bets and answered wanted ads in *Melody Maker*. He auditioned for Peter Jay and Jaywalkers, a band who did live covers of hit records when "needle time" was still restricted on the BBC. At the audition, he played The Beatles' "This Boy" and felt he had got the gig. But weeks passed and he had not heard from them. Eventually, he gave up.

At Tesco's, Alan was asked over temporarily as warehouse manager without any raise in pay. After three months, when this was not forthcoming, he walked out. It was ten days before Christmas and the seasonal rush was on. His supervisor offered to take him back, but Alan felt he had been exploited and stood his ground. Within two weeks, he found himself another job stacking shelves in a self-service convenience store in East Sheen where, the following Christmas, the boss bought him *Sergeant Pepper's Lonely Hearts Club Band* as a present. Ever a fan of the four working-class lads from Liverpool, he had saved up to buy a collarless Beatles jacket, but stopped wearing it when the Fab Four stopped wearing theirs.

By then the wholesale demolition of the slums around Notting Hill was underway and the new council blocks were rising. The Coxes too were being rehoused, out in Roehampton. There would not be room for Alan to live there with them. Instead, he rented a room in a large flat in Hammersmith, which he shared with a widow and her son – though he never saw them and kept himself to himself. He had the occasional girlfriend, but the would-be rock god now lived exclusively for the band.

Danny hired a sound studio in Denmark Street and they recorded one of Alan's songs, "I Have Seen", and "Hard Life" written by Tony and Ian. The demo was hawked around the record companies to no avail. Pop entrepreneur Don Arden, who managed the Small Faces, showed some interest in releasing it as a single and hiring The Area as a support act. But the band's equipment was stolen from the Four Feathers where the Small Faces used to practise. Luckily, Alan had taken his Höfner Verythin home with him, but he lost his amplifier. Neither Alan or the other band members could afford to replace their gear, so that was the end of The Area.

Some months later, Alan was recruited by The In-Betweens, a semi-professional band of mixed Caribbean and Asian origins, fronted by a beautiful Indo-German girl named Carmen. They played a mixture of pop and soul, and had a regular Friday-night gig in the Pied Horse in the Angel, Islington, across the road from the Post Office's Northern District sorting office where the bassist Sham Hassan worked.

In 1968, The In-Betweens were on the rise. They were gigging regularly and A&R men from the major record labels were coming to see them. They were auditioned in a studio in Shepherd's Bush. A recording contract was in prospect, along with a TV documentary about the mixed-race band. It all came to nothing when, once again, the band's equipment was stolen. This time Alan's Höfner disappeared with everything else. Again this sounded the death knell of the band.

Sham wanted Alan to form another band with him. But at a New Year's party at Linda's, Alan had met Judy Cox. Although she was also from Notting Hill, she was not related to Tony Cox's family. Four years older than Alan, she was also the offspring off a drunken, abusive father. Her mother had died when she was just sixteen-months old. While her brothers disappeared into children's homes, she had been brought up by her grandparents. Alan had met her before, briefly, when she had been studying nursing with Linda. At the time, she had been seeing an Italian trainee teacher. When she fell pregnant, he high-tailed it back to Italy, leaving her to bring up her baby daughter Natalie alone, except for the help of her aging grandmother.

Alan and Judy started dating. Despite Linda's objections – she still harboured Lily's ambition for Alan to study to be a draftsman – they decided to marry in July, a few weeks after he turned eighteen. Later he adopted Natalie, so now he had wife and child to support. After their turbulent childhoods, both of them craved stability and domesticity.

The store where he worked in East Sheen was taken over by Tesco's. Alan did not want to work for them again. He was on the lookout for another steady job when Sham suggested that he come and work with him in the Post Office. The idea appealed.

Shortly after his eighteenth birthday, Alan went for an interview at the GPO recruiting office in Lavender Hill. The General Post Office was still a government department then. It was not until the following year that the Post Office became a public corporation. In both cases, the pay was poor and there were plenty of vacancies. Alan got the job and was sent off on a two-week training course in King's Cross.

After he was married, Alan moved back into Notting Hill once more, moving into the house in Camelford Road that Judy shared with her grandmother. Thinking that her granddaughter could have done better for herself, she treated him with ill-concealed disdain.

He managed to get a posting to Barnes, a leafy suburb he had first seen on his daily bus journey from Hammersmith to East Sheen. Every morning he would cycle the five miles there, ready to start work at the crack of dawn.

On Christmas Eve 1968, Judy gave birth to their daughter Emma. Now with a growing family, Alan needed all the overtime he could get and had left behind him any idea of being a rock star. He would continue writing songs and thought he may even return to performing at some point, but he had reconciled himself to being a postman until he retired.

Chapter Six – Mr. Postman

While the Royal Mail had a huge delivery office on Barnes Green, only thirty people worked there. It was a haven of peace while the rest of the world seemed to be erupting with demonstrations against the Vietnam war and marches for civil rights. Student rebellions and the talk of revolution meant little to Alan and Judy. They were concerned with settling into respectable family life.

Barnes itself was a civilized backwater, home to established actors, artists, writers, broadcasters and the occasional government minister. As the latest recruit, Johnson's job was to cover the deliveries of men who were ill or on leave.

Young and quick on his feet, Johnson could be back in the office by 9 am, ready for a leisurely breakfast and a game of snooker in the canteen. Older hands warned him not to be so quick, otherwise more streets would be added to the round. To delay his return, he would pop across the bridge to have a cup of tea in Hammersmith which was beyond the purview of the officious inspector who checked up on the delivery men.

Most of his fellow postmen were ex-servicemen, though they never talked of their wartime experiences. One former Guardsman had previously worked as a postman in SW1. One of his duties there was to collect the parchment scrolls detailing that day's business from

Parliament and deliver it to Buckingham Palace. Johnson was impressed.

All the postmen were characters. One man claimed to have been regularly seduced on his round, which seemed unlikely. Another told of a lady who stood in her bedroom window bare-breasted each morning combing her hair. When Johnson stood in on his round one day, he discovered that this story was true.

On Johnson's first day at Barnes, he was approached by the Union of Post Office Workers and signed up, both for membership and for a UPW policy that would supplement his pension when he retired. His experience at Tesco's convinced him that he needed the protection of the union.

While the supervisor shirked his duties, Johnson was impressed with the union representative who never cut corners either in the union duties or the work he did for the post office, while earning considerably less money than his management counterpart.

While Johnson took every bit of overtime he could get – including the extra two hours he got every morning to clean the toilets – he still took time to read, now concentrating on modern history.

He also became incensed by injustices in the Post Office pay grades. The basic pay for young recruits was a pittance which, for postmen, rose to a maximum at twenty-four. But if a recruit joined at twenty-five, they would go straight on the maximum, earning considerably more than the juniors who had several years experience.

This disdain for the young extended to his work colleagues. In their heated political debates, the older postmen would brook no interjection from "juveniles" like Johnson. But while others read the *Daily Express* and the *Daily Mirror*, Johnson still read *The Times*, though he did so in secret, not to draw the fire of his comrades. He also read copies of *Newsweek* and *Punch*, slipping them temporarily from their lose paper sleeves before he delivered them.

However, he did not pay much attention to the *Post*, the union's monthly magazine, so he was surprised when the men were summoned to a union meeting and told they had been called out on a one-day strike in support of the overseas telegraph officers. They were in dispute with the management who were attempting to foist a productivity agreement on them. It was to be the union's first national strike.

The only time Alan got to voice his political opinions was with his brother-in-law, Linda's husband Mike, who he described as a "working-class Tory". While Mike condemned Enoch Powell's avowed racist "rivers of blood" speech, he supported Edward Heath's attempt to take Britain into what was then the Common Market. But when Alan spoke up in favour of the Post Office strike, Mike said it sounded as if he was on his way to become "a Bolshie shop steward".

Johnson spent the day of the strike typing up a poem for publication. He sent it to *Spring Poets '69*, a vanity publication. Inclusion cost £5 – half a week's wages. Johnson does not claim that it was a great poem, only that it was a good deal better than most of the others that had been included.

The following day, he and other men made up the day's pay they had lost, clearing the backlog on overtime. Meanwhile, the Postmaster General John Stonehouse – who later faked his own death so he could live with his mistress in Australia – offered to negotiate. *The Times* described this as "capitulation".

The union representative congratulated the staff at Barnes, but the one man who had broken the strike was sent to Coventry. No one talked to him. He was ignored. Johnson later said he felt ashamed for having colluded in his exclusion.

Five months after the strike, Johnson applied to become a Post Office driver and was sent to the driving school in Croydon. As Post Office vans did not have synchromesh gearboxes, drivers had to learn the complex technique of double declutching.

In the middle of his driving course, Johnson overslept. Fearing he would be late, he cycled furiously through the pouring rain without donning his Post Office oilskins. He arrived in the nick of time, but then passed out. His driving course was cancelled and he was sent for the medical he should have had when he first started work.

News came that Camelford Road was to be demolished. Alan and Judy were offered a council house in Slough, thirty miles west of London, while his belligerent mother-in-law was moved into sheltered accommodation.

Arriving in Slough, they were told by the local police that the Britwell Estate, where they had been offered a house, has a certain reputation for criminality. Could it be worse than the slums of Notting Hill? As they entered the estate, they saw a daub that read "Keep Britwell White." But the two-bedroom house itself, though boarded up and overgrown, was spacious and faced onto a little green. It was the sort of place Lily would have given her right arm for.

At the time, Johnson had not read John Betjeman's poem: "Come, friendly bombs, and fall on Slough!/ It isn't fit for humans now", but he had been brought up in a series of buildings that had been condemned. He knew what was fit for human habitation and what was not.

When his twelve-months probationary period with the Post Office was up, Alan got a transfer to the Slough sorting office. They moved home on 5 July 1969, the day the Rolling Stones gave a free concert in Hyde Park.

Moving in, they had no washing machine, no fridge, no vacuum cleaner and no phone. These things would have to be saved up for over many years. Memories of the tallyman coming round meant that the Johnsons eschewed buying on tick. However, there was a small coal-burning stove in the front room that, thanks to the thin walls, took the edge off the chill in the whole house. After the privations of Notting Hill, this was heaven.

Slough was a huge Post Office hub with a telephone exchange and a parcel office. The sorting office was undergoing the beginnings of automation. There was a rotating machine that separated the letters from the parcels and the sorters bundled up letters using elastic bands. In London, the men had refused to do this, tying each bundle with waxed string to avoid "de-skilling".

There were other techniques and terminology to learn and Johnson was given a week's training by Mr. Khan, an immigrant from East Pakistan, now Bangladesh. One of the first things he was told was not to leave his bicycle for a moment when delivering to his round on the Britwell Estate. Bicycles were always being stolen there. Though he found the Britwall Estate pleasant enough to live on, his round there was nowhere near as pleasant as it had been in Barnes.

The houses around the green were occupied by other young couples with children and they were soon in and out of each other's houses. Alan continued taking as much overtime as he could to support his family. This meant he saw little of them. He left for work at 5 a.m. and, after an afternoon shift in the parcels office, returned at 7.30 p.m., after the children were in bed. He regularly worked on Sundays for double time as well. Sometimes he would even cover the night shift on Fridays, working from 8 p.m. through to the end of his delivery round on Saturday.

Things improved when he managed to secure a round in the village of Burnham, which he could do on foot. It was like being back in Barnes again. Another Burnham postman would give him a lift to work in his three-wheeled Reliant Regal. Sometimes he would wake Alan, if he and Judy had been out for a few pints with the neighbours, by flinging pebbles as his bedroom window. Johnson was never a natural early riser.

Mopeds were being introduced for delivery men. Johnson got one. He then rode out to Burnham under his own steam, before beginning his rounds. It also gave him the luxury of returning home for lunch with the kids, though he never sought permission to take the moped home, figuring it must be against the rules.

The afternoon shifts in the parcels office was dirty and gruelling, but the men worked at high speed, earning themselves time to pay darts or cards for a bit before they clocked off.

When Johnson was not working or watching TV with his children, he was reading, now substituting political theory for modern history. The world then was divided ideologically between communism and capitalism; he had lived through the Cuban Missile Crisis of 1962 when the world teetered on the brink of nuclear annihilation and sought to understand why. After the serious reading was done, he still devoured the odd novel.

In the spirit of the time, he had a brief flirtation with hippydom and Judy bought him an Incredible String Band album for Christmas in 1969, along with his first razor. Although already a father, he remained a fresh-faced youth until the age of nineteen. He also found himself eligible to vote as the Representation of the People Act of 1969 reduced the age of majority in the UK from twenty-one to eighteen. He voted for the first time in 1970. While Labour held Slough, the Conservatives under Edward Heath won in the country.

A revolution was then blowing through the Post Office. The Post Office Act of 1969 abolished the position of Postmaster General and transferred his power to the new Minister of Post and

Telecommunications. He would appoint a chairman and board to run the new corporation, though it had yet to undergo the "white heat" of technological change promised by Harold Wilson in 1963.

Other things remained staunchly old-fashioned. Although there were an increasing number of Asians working for the Post Office, they sat apart from the white workers in the canteen, and there were no women workers, apart from among the casual staff taken on at Christmas.

Trouble was brewing among the ranks. After the Tory victory in 1970, the new government sacked the Post Office chairman Viscount Hall, who was thought to have been too sympathetic to the work force. As a result, there were strikes. Heath believed that he had a mandate to tame the unions. Sparks began to fly when the UPW put in a claim for a wage rise of fifteen per cent and the Post Office countered with an offer of seven. That Christmas, the union advised workers to rack up all the overtime pay they could as they would be in for a long strike in the New Year.

This was a worrying prospect for the Johnson family. There was another mouth to feed. Judy gave birth to a son, Jamie, on 10 January 1971. Alan wrote a song in celebration. There was no statutory paternity leave in those days. Johnson got his by happenstance. The UPW came out on strike on the twentieth.

Johnson was a strong supporter of the strike. The Post Office were claiming that average wages were high, but they were including overtime payments. Johnson was also suffering wage discrimination as, despite his two years' experience, he was still only twenty. The union sought to do away with the old age-related incremental scales too.

At the beginning of the strike, along with three hundred others, Johnson queued outside the benefits office in Slough. Strikers were allowed to claim for dependents, but not for themselves. Initially, Johnson was turned away – he did not appear old enough to have dependents. But when he produced his marriage certificate and the birth certificates of the children he was given £12 17s 6d a week. This was 7s 6d more than his basic wage, though not nearly as much as he got when all his overtime was added in.

None of the postmen broke the strike, but some of the telephonists, who were also members of the UPW, did. But, in Slough, the strike was a good-natured affair. Johnson and the other pickets did not shout slogans at them. They exchanged polite greetings instead.

Each week the strikers would be bussed up to Hyde Park for a rally. Johnson was not impressed by the middle-class students who tried to recruit the strikers to join the International Socialists or other far-left organizations. Johnson wanted an extra £3 a week, not a revolution. There were also local meetings in the community centre, but the debate there was largely confined to who got what from the hardship fund.

The leader of the strike was the UPW's general secretary Tom Jackson, still remembered for his huge handlebar moustache. Johnson was an instant fan. The strikers believed that they had a powerful weapon in the forthcoming Decimal Day on 15 February 1971, when the old currency of pounds, shillings and pence, with

240 pence to the pound, was to be replaced with a new one of pounds and pence, with just one hundred pence to the pound. The Post Office with its Girobank was thought to be a vital part of the changeover and, they thought, it was vital for the postal service to deliver leaflets explaining the details of the new currency.

The government had a weapon of its own. It temporarily suspended the Post Office's monopoly on postal delivery, but the private companies that stepped in proved expensive and unreliable.

Johnson was not the most militant of strikers. Though he did his share on the picket line, he spent most of his time with his children, or reading Dylan Thomas.

After seven weeks, the strike was called off. The dispute was to be settled by a committee of enquiry. There had been no vote to go out on strike. That had been an executive decision. But there was a vote to return. Johnson voted against. Nevertheless, he retained his admiration for Tom Jackson who had showed flair early in the strike when presenting the union's case to the public and the courage to lead the men back to work when he realized that the strike would inevitably end in failure. It had been the biggest industrial action, in terms of man-hours lost, since the General Strike of 1926. And to clear the backlog, there was the added bonus of unlimited overtime.

In the end, the committee of inquiry recommended a pay increase of nine per cent. However, it also adjusted the incremental scales, so Johnson himself would receive a higher hike in pay.

Chapter Seven – Part of the Union

After the strike, Johnson returned to working seven days a week, often putting in two shifts on a Sunday. His only relaxation was a drink with his neighbours on a Friday night, watching QPR's home games with a car-load of other fans from the sorting office and a kick-about on a Sunday morning as captain of South Postal FC, followed by a beer and a game of bingo, then cards, at the British Legion. After that, he took a bottle of light ale home to Judy who was cooking the Sunday lunch. Then it was off to work, or a snooze in front of the telly after watching *The Big Match*. Otherwise socializing was confined to regular house parties with neighbours, or a Saturday-night trip to a local pub, if they could get a babysitter.

After reading Dylan Thomas, Johnson became quite a fan of poetry. "Elegy Written in a Country Church Yard" had been written by Thomas Gray in St. Giles parish churchyard in Stoke Poges nearby. Johnson took Judy and the kids there for the two-hundredth anniversary of Gray's death.

Johnson returned to his drivers' training course. After five attempts, he passed his driving test and bought a Ford Anglia, which he parked proudly on the green in front of the house. This gave them the opportunity to visit family and friends.

Though he was perfectly content with being a postman for the rest of his life – he enjoyed the camaraderie – Johnson continued to strum on his Spanish guitar and write songs. Later, he bought a twelve-string Eko acoustic – not another electric guitar. This was a tacit admission that his career in rock and roll was over.

Meanwhile the pitiless routine of work still dominated his life. He got three weeks holiday a year, along with the ten days sick leave without a medical certificate that all the postmen took.

After five years in the job, Johnson was feeling a little restless. He applied for promotion to Postman Higher Grade – with a pay rise – and was sent to the Post Office training school at Bletchley Park, the home of Britain's wartime code-breakers. At the time, the code of secrecy surrounding those who had worked there had just been lifted. There he was taught the more specialist procedures he would need to know as a PHG.

But his promotion had not quelled his discontent. Back in Slough he joined the Labour Party along with his neighbour, ambulanceman Mick Pearson. Harold Wilson was then back in Downing Street, but as the head of a minority government, he was hardly in the position to continue the radical reforms he had made in his first administration.

Johnson got hold of a copy of *Das Kapital* and began studying Marxism. He had little time for the politicians in the Labour party. At the time, his political hero was Jimmy Reid, the communist trade unionist who had led a work-in at Upper Clyde Shipbuilders to victory in 1972. Reid had left school at fourteen to become a shipyard apprentice and had risen to become a national figure. But while they shared a love of music, football, books and poetry,

60

Johnson knew that the Communist Party of Great Britain was not for him. He did not see how a communist state could be a free society.

He also had discussions with the local recruiter for the Workers' Revolutionary Party, then much in vogue under the leadership of Vanessa and Corin Redgrave. It was one of the half-dozen leftist splinter groups who battled it out over ideology. While they all purported to stick up for the working class, their adherents seemed to be uniformly middle class who had no support among those they claimed to champion.

Then in 1975, Jimmy Reid quit the CPGB and joined the Labour Party, and Johnson's flirtation with the left was at an end. He now took a more active role in the union. The following February, Johnson was elected chairman of the Slough Amalgamated Branch of the Union of Post Office Workers. He managed to conclude his first AGM just as the pubs opened.

Then he set about revising the rules, insisting that the branch committees met more often and ensuring that the members were kept informed. Everything had to be done in accordance with the *ABC of Chairmanship*, written by the distinguished general secretary of the TUC, Walter Citrine. He also visited the sick and generally looked after his members.

In May 1976, he attended the annual conference of the UPW at the Winter Gardens, Bournemouth. It was the first time he had ever stayed in a hotel.

The UPW was still led by Tom Jackson who, after the comprehensive defeat of 1971, had gone on to negotiate a number of excellent pay deals. The opening session was addressed by the new Prime Minister Jim Callaghan. Six days of debate followed. Johnson enjoyed the theatre of the occasion, along with the horse-trading and the socializing.

The union opened up a new world that was far more satisfying than anything promotion in the Post Office could offer. He resigned as a PHG and went back to working long hours of overtime to make up the difference, consoling himself by taking a country round. A local newsagent paid him extra to deliver newspapers to his customers. He also delivered bags of coal, groceries and the sacks of manure to be used on the garden. One family left the cat food out, with a tin-opener, so he could feed their cat when they were away.

He attended another UPW conference at the end of 1976, but again did not pluck up the courage to speak. However, the union did present him with another opportunity – that was to continue his education. As a union official he was eligible to take any number of correspondence courses provided free of charge by the TUC. However, what correspondence courses could not teach him was the oratory that he had seen on display at union conferences.

He took the plunge at a branch meeting called over a proposed boycott of mail and telephone calls to and from South Africa after schoolchildren protesting being taught in Afrikaans had been shot down in Soweto in 1976. The anti-apartheid movement was something Johnson cared passionately about, but most of his members were against the boycott.

He addressed them in the canteen at the sorting office. It was hardly a prestigious venue and not designed for oratory. When the speech he had written was failing, he abandoned it and spoke from the heart. At the end, he received a round of applause. Nevertheless, the members voted narrowly against him.

While his love of rock music never deserted him, Johnson broadened his taste to include classical and he started a collection with Mussorgsky's *Pictures at an Exhibition*. He was soon surprised by the number of workmates who shared his new-found love of classical music and poetry.

Meanwhile, he was tireless in his union work. During his working day, Johnson would speak to his fellow postal workers and write down any complaint or comment they had in a notebook. He made a point of getting back to everyone whose criticism or remark he had logged.

Johnson's debating skills were honed in the kitchen of Hicknaham Farm where Mrs Rayham extended her hospitality to visiting tradesman. When she learnt that he was a union official, she voiced her anti-union, anti-state supported industries and anti-Common Market views. At first, Johnson was too polite to reply. Later, when a binman joined the conversation, pointing out that large European money subsidies were given to farmers, she rounded on him with detailed arguments on the importance of agriculture. Johnson soon found he could join in and such robust debates became a feature of his mornings.

His round also took in Dorneywood, the country retreat of the Home Secretary. Suspicious packages had already been winnowed out at the sorting office and, when he arrived there, he was simply waved through by the security guard. While he was never allowed inside, he would take a break there, perhaps reading a novel, before returning to do his evening collections. He enjoyed these quiet moments in the countryside as much as he did the hurly-burly of union work.

At the 1977 annual conference, there was a motion to abolish the remaining incremental scales. Although this did not affect Johnson directly, as he was now twenty-seven and on full pay, the matter still wrangled. This time he got to his feet, waved his agenda paper in the air and was called to the rostrum.

He knew that reading from a prepared script did him no favours so, instead, he had scribbled some notes on a pad he could refer to if he dried up. He presented his case, using examples from his personal experience. However, the national officer who answered his speech pointed out that pay was now subject to the all-encompassing "social contract" the unions had negotiated with the government. Consequently, minor adjustments could not be made and the conference rejected the proposal. Nevertheless, Johnson had put his toe in the water.

The following year, he decided to put his name forward for the executive council. No lesser intermediate role would do. He wanted to be in the centre of things. But he had to get the nomination of his branch and was too self-effacing to ask. Instead he accepted the position of assistant district organizer.

At the time the Callaghan government was in disarray. While it tried to fend off the demands of the unions, it was under attack by the Bennite left. Equal opportunities legislation had come into effect, allowing postwomen to join the staff at Slough. But at the Grunwick mail-order film possessing plant in Cricklewood, the workforce of mainly Asian women were trying to force union recognition. The UPW intervened, blacking the company's mail and forcing the owner to go to arbitration.

The legality of the UPW's South African boycott was still being contested. But when arbitration in the Grunwick case failed, the UPW were reluctant to re-impose the embargo for fear of further legal sanctions. However, the London District Council under John Taylor and Derek Walsh – two of Johnson's allies at conference – defied the executive and backed action by the postmen of Cricklewood, resulting in a lock-out and a mass picket of the Grunwick plant by Yorkshire miners who had been bussed in. Taylor and Walsh were then fined by the union. At that year's conference in the Winter Garden, Blackpool, Johnson spoke up for his friends.

Asked to move an amendment, Johnson approached the rostrum, only to find he was speaking to the wrong motion and had to retreat in disarray. Moments later, Tom Jackson, who had left the platform, came over to offer consolation. He also asked, in a loud voice, whether Johnson had thought of standing for the executive council. The rest of the Slough delegation were within earshot. Over lunch, they offered to nominate the following year. On his third attempt, he was elected.

In the intervening years, with Tom Jackson's encouragement, he honed his oratory. However, he found that he was not a natural showman and only found the requisite eloquence when he was talking about something he cared about. He also claimed that he did not make deals for votes in the conference bars like other candidates.

But Johnson had another political role closer to home. When Natalie failed her eleven-plus, he did not want his daughters to go to the local secondary school, Warrenfield Comprehensive, which had a bad reputation. Instead, he got her into Haymill, where he became a school governor. Then came the news that the school had been earmarked for closure and he joined the fight to save it – though this eventually failed.

He gave up smoking and used the money he saved to extend his record collection – even venturing into punk with albums by Elvis Costello and Joe Jackson. Meanwhile, the political landscape was changing. Callaghan's government was plagued by the "winter of discontent" and in March 1979 it lost a vote of confidence in the House of Commons. The ensuing election that May brought Margaret Thatcher to power.

Active in the local Labour Party, Johnson got to know the local MP, Joan Lestor, and drove her around during the campaign. The front room of the Johnsons' house was used as a Labour committee room on polling day. While until then he had only interested himself in political theory, now he saw the mechanics of getting the vote out.

Once Johnson had been elected to the executive committee of what was now called the Union of Communication Works in May 1981, he quit the sorting office. His early morning rounds were now over. He was now on permanent special leave from the Post Office to go about his union business.

Before his first meeting of the executive committee, Johnson found himself in the room alone with Tom Jackson. He had already sent a note of congratulation. Now he said he had high hopes for Johnson's future in the union.

The union's headquarters were in Clapham, an hour's drive from Slough. He would have an office there. Otherwise he was to teach at the union training schools, help resolve disputes, support national officers in their negotiations and attend conferences of sister unions around the world as a fraternal delegate.

Following the fall of the Callaghan government, Labour was under attack by a group of Trotskyite insurgents known as Militant tendency, formerly the Revolutionary Socialist League. They trashed anyone connected with the previous administration, with the exception of Tony Benn. Johnson found Benn articulate and persuasive, and agreed with a lot he had to say. But his refusal to stick up for former colleagues smacked of treachery, Johnson thought.

The Post Office was already under attack from Mrs. Thatcher who wanted the London postal service investigated by the Monopolies and Mergers Commission. The management and union had to find some way to reform some of the more dubious working practices before the commission wrote its report. As a result, Improved Working Methods were introduced, which traded reductions in overtime against weekly bonuses.

Johnson convinced Slough to participate in this scheme. It seemed to him that this gave the workers a measure of control and introduced a form of what was then known as industrial democracy. While this was being discussed at the executive committee, Johnson discovered that he was the only member who knew how things actually worked in a sorting office. Consequently, Tom Jackson asked Johnson to give seminars and write a handbook, explaining IWM – though there was still considerable opposition to it throughout the ranks.

Chapter Eight – Moving On Up

Life had changed for Alan Johnson. He now wore a suit to work, just as his mother had always wanted him to. Soon he was to make his first flight on an aeroplane, when he was on his way to resolve a strike in Dundee involving the new IWM scheme.

Having mastered the details of IWM, he found it relatively easy to solve the dispute and returned south the next day with a Dundee cake and book of Robbie Burns' verse.

With the introduction of postcodes across the country, mechanization was now coming to the Post Office. But Johnson had other concerns. A kick-around with two youngsters resulted in a broken ankle, bring a premature end to his footballing career at the age of just thirty-one. This also kept him out of the office and away from resolving disputes for six weeks. However, the time off allowed him to get on with writing the IWM handbook Tom Jackson had asked him for. It was published as *The Step-by-Step Guide to IWM*. The scheme worked well enough to see off the Monopolies and Mergers Commission and, for the moment, the Post Office was safe.

Political discord was provoked locally by the Thatcher government's "right to buy" scheme. The scheme gave the Johnsons and their neighbours the right to buy their houses from the council as a discount. It was a matter of fierce debate. Alan was against it. He argued that, if they exercised their right to buy, they would be depriving future generations of the chance of having their own council house – the one thing that Lily had always dreamed of. In discussions, he generally found himself on the wrong side of the argument. Most of his neighbours bought their houses, then sold up and moved away. But the Johnsons clung onto their house and their principles.

Besides Johnson's home in Slough was handy for Heathrow airport and he became a frequent flier. He flew regularly to Northern Ireland to hold seminars and weekend courses though the Troubles were raging there. It was dangerous work as the UCW was determinedly non-sectarian and, out on the streets, postal workers were particularly vulnerable.

In 1982, Johnson drove Tom Jackson to the union meeting at Ascot where he was to announce that he was stepping down as general secretary. Other senior members of the union were also due to retire and, on the way back to London, Jackson told him that he should aim to become General Secretary. But first he would have to become a union national officer. He would have to watch his back, Jackson warned. Others had ambitions to be General Secretary and the knives were already drawn.

Johnson now had his job cut out extending the IWM scheme to parts of the country that were reluctant to embrace it. He had to travel around the nation trying to convince the recalcitrant. He also held seminars to explain the complex formulas involved, though he was a dunce at maths at school himself. Fortunately, the electronic calculator had just been introduced.

A training school was set up in a hotel the union had bought in Bournemouth. But other members of the executive committee studiously avoided it, so Johnson had the field to himself. However, his efforts won favour with the rank and file. He placated the regional managers and won the members substantial pay increases and sometimes a large lump sum covering arrears. Soon he was topping the polls in the annual executive committee elections and the ballots for the TUC and Labour Party conference delegations.

He attended the Labour Party conference for the first time in 1982. Michael Foot was leader. Johnson was an admirer, especially of his masterful two-volume biography of Aneurin Bevan, though Foot was clearly the wrong man to be leading the party into the election the following year. And that election was to be crucial. Mrs. Thatcher was already bringing in laws to curb the unions. The closed shop was to be outlawed. Strike ballots became mandatory and General Secretaries were to stand for election every five years – to be fair, a measure the postal union had already considered and rejected. Under the Thatcher government, the consensual approach to industrial relations that had operated since World War II had been thrown out of the door and the unions were under siege.

The postal union was particularly vulnerable. In 1981, telecommunications – that is, the telephone, what was left of the telegraph and other wire-based systems – had been hived off from the Post Office. Then in 1982, the government announced it was to be privatized and the field would be opened up to competition from other telecommunications companies. This went ahead after the Conservatives' landslide victory in 1983 when even Joan Lestor lost her seat. By then, Johnson was the executive of Labour's southern region, where the party came in third, behind the Conservatives and the upstart SDP-Liberal Alliance, which later became the Liberal Democrats after a poor showing in the 1987 election.

As the heads of the trade unions no longer had access to power, the members of the UCW became restive, while the officials became involved in infighting. Things became worse for the unions in the mid-1980s, when the miners' strike was soundly defeated and Rupert Murdoch broke the print unions in Fleet Street. And while the UCW opposed the privatization of British Telecom in 1984, its members bought shares.

Trade unionists were under attack from the other side too. While they wore smart suits when representing their members at Labour Party conferences, they found themselves surrounded by youths wearing denim, covered in badges supporting all manner of far-left causes. Only Arthur Scargill and the NUM executive drew applause, but it was clear that they had led their troops over a cliff.

While it was hoped that the Post Office itself was safe from the rising tide of privatization, it was divided up into four sectors – mails, counters, parcels and the Girobank. The union feared this might be the first step towards a sell-off. The only card the union was holding was that the Post Office actually made money for the Exchequer. But clearly to fend off Mrs. Thatcher, the union would have to make peace with management, so they could present a united front to the government.

Johnson was privy to the talks and watched the new general secretary Alan Tuffin, a master negotiator, in action. Sitting beside Tuffin, Johnson said that he learnt the necessity of earning the respect of the opponent, listening carefully to their arguments and using delaying tactics, such as adjournments, to think things over rather that make hasty decisions.

The upshot of the talks was an agreement called Safeguarding the Future of the Mails Business. Under it, IWM, now seen as his baby, was to be extended and Johnson got much of the credit.

Johnson's duties kept away from home a lot. He even travelled abroad to meetings of the PTTI – the Postal, Telegraph and Telephone International. Domestically, he and other members of the executive were involved in fire-fighting exercises, trying to quell the spontaneous walkouts, by then illegal, caused by the over-zealous imposition of the SFMB agreement.

In those days, wild-cat strikes were common. One was caused by the arrest of a sixty-year-old sorter after an officious Post Office manager in Preston had seen him briefly examining a holiday brochure that had been in the post. Every postal worker in the north-west walked out. Johnson was called in to sort out the situation.

In talks, the Post Office conceded that this was hardly a criminal matter. It would be handled by a disciplinary hearing where the offender would be represented by Johnson, who had already made a secret agreement that no action would result. Everyone went back to work. In such encounters, Johnson earned the trust of both the management and the workforce.

To fulfil his ambition of becoming General Secretary, he still had to become a national officer. Despite his popularity among the membership, twice he was beaten in the polls for vacant offices.

Johnson was at the Labour Party conference in Bournemouth in 1985, when leader Neil Kinnock took on Militant, saying famously: "You start with far-fetched resolutions. They are then pickled into a rigid dogma, a code, and you go through the years sticking to that, out-dated, misplaced, irrelevant to the real needs, and you end in the grotesque chaos of a Labour council – a *Labour* council! – hiring taxis to scuttle round a city handing out redundancy notices to its own workers. I'm telling you… you can't play politics with people's jobs and people's services."

This caused acrimony with the part, Even the branch in Slough had its Militant cadre. Although Johnson was a man of the left, he had little time for the firebrands on the rostrum who could not negotiation or advance the cause of the working class in any practical way.

Rather than taking political postures, the UCW tried to co-operate with the government to advance the interests of its members. It helped persuade the Post Office to accept money from the failing Youth Training Scheme to set up a Postal Cadet Scheme, guaranteeing jobs to sixteen-year-olds, though union activists, particularly those in the north, were against it. Johnson was sent to talk them round – with limited success.

When the quaintly named position of "outdoor secretary" became open, Johnson was asked to step in temporarily. And when a ballot was held, he was elected permanently to the position. Then, at last, he quit the Post Office and became an full-time employee of the union.

As his union work took up so much of his time, it was inevitable that Alan and Judy grew apart. While his life was full of travel and new challenges, she had remained at home. The children had grown up and, without him around, she had grown lonely. They talked it over and decided that it was better if they split up. After the couple divorced in 1991, Johnson married Laura Jane Patient. They had a son in 2000.

Chapter Nine – The World of Politics

Alan Johnson's career in the union continued without a hitch. In January 1992, he was elected General Secretary, the youngest in its history. Then when the government announced that it intended to privatize the Post Office, he turned the tables on them by hiring the Tories own PR guru Tim Bell – the man behind the 1979 "Labour Isn't Working" campaign – to trash the plans. As a result, the Royal Mail remained in public hands for the time being.

From his position as General Secretary, Johnson threw his net wider, becoming a director of Unity Trust Bank plc and a member of Ruskin College Oxford's governing council. He served on the General Council of the TUC and was a member of the National Executive Committee. He was also a member of the World Executive of PTTI which the UCW was affiliated to.

In 1995, he oversaw the Union of Communications Workers' merger with the National Communications Union to form the Communications Workers' Union and became its first Joint General Secretary. By then, Johnson was a political insider as a member of Labour's National Executive. Broadly seen as a Blairite, he was an advocate of modernization of the party. He was the only leader of a major union to champion the abolition of Clause Four of Labour Party Constitution that promised "the common ownership of the means of production, distribution and exchange". He even drafted a pamphlet for the Fabian Society that suggested ways the unions could loosen their links with the Labour Party.

A few months before the 1997 general election, he was approached by Tony Blair, who offered him a safe seat. Stuart Randall, the MP for West Hull and Hessle where he commanded an impregnable nine thousand majority, suddenly stood down and was subsequently elevated to the House of Lords. Johnson was parachuted in and won the seat with an increased major as Blair swept to victory.

As a back-bench MP, Johnson took an £11,000 pay cut, stepping down from his £54,000-a-year position as General Secretary of the CWU. Nevertheless, he was tipped for greater things.

"Alan is the most able union leader of his generation and Tony wanted him," said a Labour spokesman. "He will be a first class MP and a brilliant minister – he won't be a backbencher for long."

He made his maiden speech in the House of Commons about the long campaign for trawlermen's compensation, which he eventually led to success three years later. He also took up the case of the trawler *Gaul*, which sank in the North Sea in 1974 amid allegations that she was spying. This resulted in a new formal investigation in 2004.

One of Johnson's first jobs after being elected to parliament was to head the investigation into allegations that Mohammed Sarwar, the MP for Glasgow Govan, gave a bribe to another candidate in the general election campaign. Meanwhile, the Fabian pamphlet Johnson had written was dropped quietly in the bin.

He was appointed parliamentary private secretary to Dawn Primarolo, then Financial Secretary to the Treasury. It was not a marriage made in heaven. Primarolo was known as "Red Dawn" and had petitioned the Soviet government to rehabilitate Leon Trotsky. After his appointment, the *Sunday Mirror* awarded Johnson their "Worst Joke of the Year" award, when he quipped: "This is the era of a new Dawn."

He continued as her PPS when she became Paymaster General. But this position was a stepping stone. In 1999, he became a minister in the Department of Trade and Industry. From there he moved to the Department for Education and Skills as Minister for Higher Education. Many thought this was a strange appointment as he had left school at fifteen. However, he proved a cunning and persuasive campaigner in the battle to get the back benches to support "top up" university tuition fees. He argued that in forty years of free higher education the social class gap had widened rather than narrowed. Graduates should make a contribution to their degree course – £1 in every £14 spent – to help fund the expansion of higher education. He also urged the return of maintenance grants for the poorest students.

Although he did not have an O-level to his name, Johnson cut a more convincing figure among old Labour stalwarts than Charles Clarke, his hectoring, public-school-educated boss.

"I was part of the charm offensive with Charles Clarke," Johnson said. "I did the charming and he was offensive."

Before the vote, the Labour whips were so unsure of victory that Blair discussed the terms of the motion of confidence that would have followed such a major defeat.

Thanks to Johnson, the measure was carried, but by just five votes. Blair rewarded him with a Cabinet post as Secretary of State for Work and Pensions, making him the first ex-union General Secretary to join the Cabinet since Frank Cousins in 1964.

It was not an easy position to step into. The Child Support Agency was in virtual meltdown and there was a £50 billion shortfall in the nation's pensions provision – some twelve million people were not saving enough for their retirement. But when the subject was debated in the House of Commons, Johnson crushed the Tories' spokesman David Willetts, citing Labour's achievement of lifting two million pensioners out of abject poverty. Meanwhile he showed a killer instinct when he threw the Child Support Agency boss, Doug Smith, to the wolves on live television in front of a House of Common's select committee.

Following that performance, there was talk of his possible leadership candidacy when Tony Blair stood down. It was said that he was being groomed for the top job by the "Anyone But Brown" caucus.

"Don't put money on it," he told the press. "It's science fiction – but nice science fiction. I got rid of my leadership tendencies in the Communication Workers Union. I've got it out of my system. I wanted to get to the top there. I don't really want to get to the top here. It's just fantasy."

The job he really wanted, he said, was to be manager of Queen's Park Rangers. At the time, it was noted, he was reading Roy Jenkins' biography of Churchill, perhaps picking up a few tips on late-developing political careers.

After the Labour Party won a third term in 2005, Johnson became Secretary of State for Trade and Industry – he was to have been Productivity, Energy and Industry Secretary until someone realized that the acronym would have spelt out "PENIS".

In the reshuffle the following year, he became Secretary of State for Education and Skills. In this role, he urged parents to play a bigger role in their child's education with his "Every Parent Matters" strategy. He said parenting had been a "no go" area for government, but people needed help. Research had shown that three-quarters of parents wanted advice on bringing up their children.

From his own experience, Johnson believed that one of the most important things a parent could do to boost their children's chances in life was to read to them. This was a simple solution, he said, "but in a busy world it doesn't happen enough. Thirty per cent of parents don't read regularly with their children – a vital but missed opportunity to boost their children's development. We watch an average of four hours television a day. If we read to children for just a tenth of this every day, we'd give their chances a massive boost."

He gave his backing to the National Year of Reading the following year, hoping it would bring about a step change in attitudes to reading for advancement and pleasure.

"Reading opens up a world of opportunities and books are the foundation on which we can build other learning," he said. "Reading should be a source of pleasure in itself, as well as an essential support for increasing the life chances of children."

This certainly echoed his own life experience.

Extra advice and support was to be offered to parents with numeracy and literacy problems, encouraging them to participate in learning activities with their children. A particular effort was made to get working parents, especially fathers, to be more involved with their children. Schemes highlighted by Johnson include one where fathers worked with their children on allotments, visited sports facilities together or took part in music projects. However, the parenting strategy, he said, had to be "bias-free", adding: "It's what parents do, not who they are, that makes the difference."

Johnson had already opened up a debate about the role of the family after the then leader of the opposition David Cameron suggested fathers should be forced to support their children and Prime Minister Tony Blair called for "intervention" at an early age to tackle problem children. While refusing to stigmatize "alternative lifestyles" or single parents, there has been an underlying agreement between the political parties that the traditional family structure of a married mother and father raising children was the best option. Johnson challenged this assumption head on, suggesting that other family models could be equally effective and that there was nothing essentially superior about the traditional unit.

"While marriage represents the pinnacle of a strong relationship," he said, "that does not mean that all children from married couples fare well, nor that every other kind of alternate family structure is irretrievably doomed to fail."

He argued that the debate centring around marriage was looking at the issue through the wrong end of the telescope.

"It's the child that is at the centre of this, it's the parenting that matters, it's not the form of the relationship," he said.

He particularly attacked Cameron's suggestion that tax breaks to encourage marriage were the way forward.

"It's wrong to suggest that tax and legislation makes relationships, it's not, it's love," he said.

He also branded the old married couples' allowance, abolished by Labour, as "pernicious and judgmental" because it discriminated against the third of all children whose parents are not married.

Nevertheless, he was at odds with Tony Blair, who continued to urge that "marriage is good". This was seen as the opening in Johnson's bid to become deputy leader when John Prescott stepped down.

Johnson also warned of the dangers of the new system of diplomas that the government were introducing, telling the Association of School and College Leaders conference: "Things could go horribly wrong, particularly as we are keeping A-levels and GCSEs. The decision was taken in the interests of diversity, so young people have choice. That does mean there is a danger of the diplomas becoming, if you like, the secondary modern compared to the grammar."

This drew fire from the chair of the Commons education select committee, Labour MP Barry Sheerman.

"I don't think it is for the secretary of state to spread alarm and despondency," he said. "I would prefer the secretary of state to lead from the front and accentuate the positives – get off his backside and do something about it."

But the general secretary of the ASCL called Johnson's comments "refreshingly honest".

He got teachers on side by recommending a new pay structure for part-time teachers, giving them the same contractual conditions as their full-time colleagues. This meant that part-time teachers in England and Wales would be paid for work they did outside the class, such as preparing lessons and marking.

After standing aside in the race to become leader of the party, saying he was backing the favourite Gordon Brown, Johnson stood in the contest for deputy leader.

"It is, of course, a matter for the party to decide who the leader's going to be, but my view is Gordon is a towering political figure," he said. "It's not a position that I ever sought and there is a superb candidate in Gordon Brown."

As a deputy leader, he said, he hoped to "complement, help, cajole and assist" the party leader and occasionally tell them what they do not want to hear. "I think that's an important role and that's one I want to put myself forward for."

Johnson received the most nominations for the post and led the ballot in the first four rounds of voting. But in the fifth he was pipped at the post by Harriet Harman, who won by just 0.8 per cent.

Self-effacing as ever, Johnson said he was not disappointed for himself, but was disappointed for his campaign team. Ms. Harman would be a "very good deputy leader," he said. "I think there was a big view in the party that it needed to be a woman."

When Gordon Brown took over as Prime Minister in June 2007 he made Johnson Secretary of State for Health. The following year, he found himself embroiled in the controversy over breast-cancer-sufferer Debbie Hirst who was warned that she would be denied treatment on the NHS if she sold her house to buy the expensive anti-cancer drug Avastin. Johnson supported the NHS position, saying that patients "cannot, in one episode of treatment, be treated on the NHS and then allowed, as part of the same episode and the same treatment, to pay money for more drugs". It was, he said, against "a founding principle of the NHS... that someone is either a private patient or an NHS patient".

He also ran into difficulties when Maidstone & Tunbridge Wells NHS Trust agreed to pay £250,000 compensation to their chief executive after sacking her over an outbreak of C.difficile in their hospitals. Johnson intervened, blocking the payment. However, the payment went ahead after the case reached the court of appeal.

In June 2009, he was appointed Home Secretary. Now he could return to Dorneywood, this time as a resident. But almost immediately he was involved in controversy when he sacked

Professor David Nutt as chairman of the Advisory Council of the Misuse of Drugs.

Professor Nutt had claimed that ecstasy, LSD and cannabis were less dangerous than alcohol and tobacco.

"Alcohol ranks as the fifth most harmful drug after heroin, cocaine, barbiturates and methadone. Tobacco is ranked ninth," he wrote in the paper from the centre for crime and justice studies at King's College, London. "Cannabis, LSD and ecstasy, while harmful, are ranked lower at eleventh, fourteenth and eighteenth respectively."

He complained that politicians were distorting and devaluing evidence supplied by research into illicit drugs after the previous Home Secretary, Jaqui Smith, had reclassified cannabis from Class C to Class B, ignoring the recommendations of his committee, and rejecting the scientific advice to downgrade MDMA from Class A.

Alan Johnson wrote to Professor Nutt, saying: "It is important that the government's messages on drugs are clear and as an advisor you do nothing to undermine public understanding of them. As my lead advisor on drug harms I am afraid the manner in which you have acted runs contrary to your responsibilities. I cannot have public confusion between scientific advice and policy and have therefore lost confidence in your ability to advise me as Chair of the ACMD. I would therefore ask you to step down with immediate effect."

Johnson's position worsened over the next few months as another seven members of the ACMD quit, complaining that decisions on the classification of drug mephedrone were made due to media and political pressure.

"There's not been proper consideration given to the broader justice and political aspects of making a drug Class B and criminalizing maybe tens of thousands of young people," Johnson said. "I'm not surprised that people think it's all been done for political reasons rather than scientific or health reasons."

Shadow Home Secretary Chris Grayling said the relationship between the government and the ACMD had become "utterly shambolic", but reserved faint praise for Johnson.

"After all the chaos of the last few months, it finally looked as if Alan Johnson might be getting things back into shape again," he said. "The decision on mephedrone was the right one, but this latest resignation suggests pretty clearly that the Home Secretary has been completely unable to restore his relationship with the experts who advise him."

When British resident and former Guantanamo Bay detainee Binyam Mohamed claimed that MI5 officers had fed questions to his CIA torturers in Pakistan and Morocco, Johnson warned that any police investigation into the matter could jeopardize Britain's national security. He said the claims were "baseless, groundless accusations". The courts did not agree. Binyam Mohamed was given £1 million in compensation by the government, rather than investigating the matter further.

Despite these political difficulties, key members of the Cabinet suspected Johnson of plotting to unseat Gordon Brown.

"However, he steadfastly denied he was interested in the top job, and on more than one occasion stated he did not feel he was up to it," said the *Sunday Telegraph*. "Despite this lack of ambition, several Labour MPs thought his easy going manner would make him a more popular leader than Mr Brown, particularly in marginal seats in the south of England, and would give the party a better chance of retaining power in this year's election. Several urged him to oppose Mr Brown."

Nevertheless, he remained loyal into the 2010 election and beyond.

Chapter Ten – Into the Wilderness

In May 2010 the Labour government was swept from office, but Johnson stayed on the front bench as Shadow Home Secretary. Despite this electoral setback, he still appeared to be the coming man in the Labour Party. Within a week, the *London Evening Standard* were tipping Alan Johnson to be a candidate to take on Boris Johnson in the election to be Mayor of London which was still two years away. It would be "Johnson versus Johnson," the paper said.

Alan Johnson was well qualified for the job. A Londoner born and bred, he was a "big-hitter" from the Blair-Brown Cabinet. And he was certainly available. He had already backed out of the forthcoming leadership race, saying it was time for the "next generation" of politicians to take up the fight against the Conservatives nationally and backing David Miliband for the post.

According to the *Standard*: "Allies of the former Home Secretary would love to see a 'Johnson v Johnson' contest and believe their man is the type of big figure needed to knock out Boris. A skilled media performer, AJ's easy charm and quick wit would ensure a mouth-watering clash with Bojo. But he also has impeccable Londoner credentials.

"Born and bred in Notting Hill when it was an impoverished collection of tenements rather than the Cameroonian haven it is today, he was brought up by his teenage sister after his mother died.

He then became a London postie – and can still remember the streets he pounded across the city – before rising to become leader of the postal workers' union and then an MP."

He did not take the bait and backed Oona King instead. After Ken Livingston won the nomination, there was speculation that the new Labour leader Ed Miliband might deselect Livingston and put Johnson in his place. Livingston was sceptical.

"Alan Johnson is a lovely fellow," he said, "but to do this you have to be absolutely ruthless, relentless, and driven. No one ever accused Alan of that."

Johnson later revealed that he had never considered running for Mayor of London. He was the MP for Hull and that was where his allegiance lay. Nor would he run for mayor in 2016 as he wanted to stay on as an MP.

By then, he had withdrawn from frontline politics. After Labour's defeat in 2010, he threw himself behind the campaign for electoral reform. He wrote an article for the *Observer* condemning Nick Clegg for going into the coalition without insisting on some form of proportional representation.

The following month, the *Sunday Telegraph* were saying that Labour's "lost leader" was considering standing down from his Westminster seat and fighting a by-election on the issue of proportional representation.

"Mr. Johnson, who was the favoured candidate of many Labour MPs to replace Gordon Brown as prime minister, has always been a passionate advocate of electoral reform," the paper said.

In the run-up to the Labour leadership contest, he told the *Hull Daily Mail*: "I may not put myself forward for the shadow cabinet elections and am thinking about going on to the back benches. I might be able to do something from the sidelines on the proportional representation issue. I think this is a real time of progress on that."

Fellow Labour MPs thought any attempt to force a by-election was risky. In 2008, Conservative Shadow Home Secretary David Davis had resigned and forced a by-elector on the issue of the erosion of civil liberties.

"It's hard to see that Alan would do something like that," said one Labour MP. "It sounds barking. David Davis did it and put a giant dent in his career. Having said that, Alan is absolutely a hundred per cent committed to voting reform and I suppose he might just be tempted into a grand gesture."

He didn't. But he did support the "Yes to fairer votes" campaign in the run-up to the referendum on 5 May 2011, appearing on the platform of the headline London event alongside Ed Miliband.

Despite being the first MP to back David Miliband in the leadership election, in October 2010, Johnson was invited by Ed Miliband to join his first Shadow Cabinet as Shadow Chancellor, over Ed Balls and his wife Yvette Cooper. Both Balls, who had been a leadership contender, and Cooper, who had topped the Shadow Cabinet poll, had been tipped for the job.

Johnson quickly demonstrated that he was a Miliband loyalist.

"Since his election as leader, Ed has demonstrated real strength of character and determination to unify and lead," he told the press.

91

"We are both passionate about a new kind of politics where we will not disagree with our political opponents for the sake of it. These are testing times and we will be a responsible opposition acting in the national interest… Ed and I will work together to build a plan for growth and for jobs in our economy. We will offer a real and responsible alternative to the dangerous plans of this coalition government, which is damaging the economic future of millions of families."

In his first major speech in the post, he advocated an extra levy on bankers of £3.5 billion. Conservative proposal, he said, "meant families take the strain while bankers grab the bonuses. There's no justification for such an unfair sharing of the burden."

However, Johnson was clearly ill-suited to the job. The BBC reported that "his economic credentials had been brought into question after several recent gaffes. In an interview he appeared not to know the rate of National Insurance paid by employers, and he was also reported to have clashed with his party leader over the policy of introducing a graduate tax to replace university tuition fees."

After less than four months in the job, Johnson stood down, citing personal reasons. He had discovered that his wife had been having an affair with his police bodyguard while he had been Home Secretary.

Johnson issued a statement saying: "I have found it difficult to cope with personal issues in my private life while carrying out an important front bench role."

He told the *Hull Daily Mail* that sorting out problems in his personal life was more important than fighting the Government over the economy.

"I don't think that I could have coped properly," he said. "You know you have to do your job properly. If you are trying to deal with your job as an MP, deal with your job as a frontbench spokesman in the shadow cabinet and shadow chancellor and at the same time you have got lots of problems to sort out at home, you can't do all three. You have to think about that and I thought, I am going to stay being a member of parliament. I need to sort our personal problems, so the shadow chancellor's position had to go."

Labour leader Ed Miliband told the BBC he had accepted his resignation "with great regret" and deputy leader Harriet Harman told BBC Radio 4's Today programme that Johnson's departure was "a very sad loss to our front bench in the Labour Party but I also think he's a loss to frontline British politics. He was universally liked and admired and we will very much miss him."

Even David Cameron was sympathetic.

"Obviously, I am very sorry for Alan because he has given a huge amount of service in public life, on the frontline," he said. "He's one of the more cheerful and optimistic characters in politics. I am sure he will go on doing a good job for his constituents and being an MP, and I hope he is able to sort out all the things he wants to. We will miss him on the front bench."

The *Independent* pointed out that, while it was relatively common for politicians to be forced out of office because they have been caught cheating on their wives, Johnson was the first to resign because of a looming sex scandal in which he was the aggrieved party.

Johnson later admitted that he did not like the job of Shadow Chancellor and was surprised when Ed Miliband had offered it to him.

"I was glad to get out," he said. "I took it because I thought, 'What an extraordinary gesture, that he wants me there'. But my heart wasn't in it. I didn't like the job."

He was replaced by Gordon Brown's former Treasury advisor Ed Balls.

Johnson's protection officer PC Paul Rice was suspended from duty and later dismissed from police service following an internal investigation and a misconduct hearing. Johnson defended his "poor wife" who he said was upset by all the attention created by the scandal. She was granted a divorce in 2014, after two years separation.

Johnson had moved on, starting a new relationship with fifty-year-old award-winning businesswoman who was the boss of translation agency Language is Everything in Hull. He revealed the relationship in a local newspaper interview celebrating award of the MBE for services to business and the Humber area.

After Johnson's divorce Ed Miliband approached him and asked him if he was interested in returning to front-line politics. Johnson said no.

"What about freelancing?" asked Miliband.

"I am happy to go round the country, campaigning, talking to parties," he said, though he was frustrated that Labour had not been more effective in attacking Chancellor George Osbourne over the economy. Miliband, he said, should make "a couple of big speeches... just taking the whole thing apart".

By then, Johnson had embarked on a literary career. The first volume of his autobiography, *The Boy: A Memoir of Childhood*, published in 2013, won the Royal Society of Literature's Ondaadtje Prize for a literary work "evoking the spirit of a place" and the Orwell prize for political writing, beating Charles Moore's account of Mrs. Thatcher's early life.

In a review in the *Guardian*, former MP Chris Mullin said the book was "the biography of a politician like no other... from time to time, one has to pinch oneself to recall that this is not an account of childhood in Victorian England, but of life in the England of the 1950s and 60s. Far from being a misery memoir, it is beautifully observed, humorous, moving, uplifting; told with a dry, self-deprecating wit and not a trace of self-pity."

Accepting the prize, Johnson said that he had set out to "recapture north Kensington from Notting Hill", noting that "Julia Roberts and Hugh Grant were not often seen down our way... People lived sixteen in a house, but you were forced into a community, and were looking after people who couldn't look after themselves."

The second volume of his autobiography, *Please, Mr Postman*, was published in 2014. The *Independent* said that the book was "a wonderful elegy for a life that has only just passed into history. A time when nobody drank at home, when Post Office vans required double de-clutching and when the 'fax machine – believe it or not – was seen as a serious threat to our future'."

In it, he looks back at a time when the strike-happy officials in his own union were "like pilots who knew how to take off but who'd never been taught to land". He also points out that Arthur Scargill may have been right about the Coal Board's plan to close pits. But, he says: "The job of a trade-union leader isn't to predict rain, it's to build a bloody ark."

In it he gives a clue to why his advancement up the political ladder was so slow and why he did not have the ruthlessness to seize the top job when it was within his grasp.

"My personality was steeped in the self-effacement that held back so many working-class people," he said.

But then, Alan Johnson has read Roy Jenkins' biography of Winston Churchill and knows that Churchill did not become Prime Minster for the first time until he was sixty-five. He still claimed to be bereft of ambition. Being Prime Minister is a "godawful job," Johnson said. Nor was he planning to revive his musical career, saying that he had not touched a guitar for the ten years he had been in Cabinet.

What drove Alan Johnson was never a hunger for power. The final tribute should come from his sister, Linda, who said he inherited his decency and determination to fight for others from their mother.

"I remember remarking on the sense of justice and fairness he'd inherited from Mum," she said. "Even though we could have gone off the rails when Mum died, we were doing exactly what she would have wanted – making a difference to the people around us. She would be extremely proud of him for getting where he is today."